STOP

This is the back of the book! Start from the other side.

NATIVE MANGA
readers read manga from _right to left_.

If you run into our **Native Manga** logo on any of our books... you'll know that this manga is published in it's true original native Japanese right to left reading format, as it was intended. Turn to the other side of the book and start reading from right to left, top to bottom.

Follow the diagram to see how its done.
Surf's Up!

READ RIGHT TO LEFT

Chapter 1

For years before I came to settle here in Umbria, the name conjured up for me a strange, wild, contradictory place. Despite travelling the length and breadth of mainland Italy numerous times, tunnelling through as many veins and arteries as its railway system dictated, I never reached the lungs: the self-seeded Umbrian forests. I had heard that there were bears and wolves in Umbria, and hideaways in the woods where kidnap victims were held by their Sardinian captors. It was said to be a poor, infertile place where life was hard for the *contadini* who slaved for their feudal overlords, who were, in turn, the bastard sons of cardinals and popes.

My family and I were in Italy house-hunting. We had been looking for a suitably dilapidated villa for three years. With such a serious task before us, we had no time for sightseeing, so the old Papal States remained a mystery on the periphery of our half-hearted search. Half-hearted in the sense that we rarely visited a house, villa, tower or farm. Most of our efforts centred on bars, where we would sit and discuss what we were looking for. Each winter, this dream house would be taken back to whichever ill-heated rented place we were then living in, and used to fan the meagre flames of the fire we huddled around.

I had a mental picture of my ideal house which I had

been carrying around with me like a piece of luggage since my schooldays. It had been to Venezuela and back through the Caribbean. It had travelled with me to North America and Canada and as far south as Patagonia. I took it from frontier to frontier across Europe. I wanted a house so huge that I could move from room to empty room without disturbing anyone. The design of the house was as fickle as most young loves, and changed in shape and layout all the time. The only constant features in my dream image were a pillared loggia, a stone arch, a terracotta balustrade and a line of sentinel cypresses.

Another detail of this lovely villa was that it had to roughly match my budget and clock in at under the price of a simple, three-bedroomed apartment in the provinces. To this end, I kept a piggy-bank, which I continually raided and refilled. But the years of pursuit of the grand *palazzo* finally ate into my funds to such a degree that its dilapidation had to increase in direct proportion to the vanishing savings. None of the villas, houses or cottages hitherto produced by eager estate agents had been even remotely viable, short of joining in the popular Italian sport of holding up banks.

One of the large blue trunks that travelled around with me from station to station gathering knocks and labels as it accompanied my family circus was reserved exclusively for unanswered letters and miscellaneous papers. Among these was a sheaf of brochures on properties for sale in Umbria. Although none of the houses advertised had ever sounded suitable (or cheap) enough to visit, I had kept the leaflets with all the other junk I saved and carried with me in lieu of the familiarity of a home. Of these properties, the most interesting was a twelfth-century castle where a Holy Roman Emperor had lived. I gradually accumulated a dossier on this castle. I had everything but a photograph. Three years went by and there was still no better picture

2

than a blurred photocopy of a long row of what looked like stone pigsties with an arch in the middle. This, I was told, was the back; the front towered up through many floors and was a fantastic spectacle. There was (supposedly) a Roman amphitheatre, a great hall, an inner courtyard, a vaulted stable and an underground tunnel, all going for a song. The castle had everything, in fact, to stir the imagination except a photo; and what with one thing and another, we never went to look.

Meanwhile, unable to find a house, my husband, Robbie Duff-Scott, and I moved to Venice with my adolescent daughter, the child Iseult, and my small son, Allie. The need for a vast villa waned, and the search was temporarily suspended. The nearest I had to an Italian garden were the eight windowsills of our apartment, which I disputed with a number of ailing and incontinent pigeons. For the first time in four years we had our own base. We were cramped but happy. Robbie is a painter of large canvases and needs a lot of studio space. And, I have the makings of a bag lady in me, with my habit of hoarding everything. The children, like good Venetians, appropriated the rest of the city for their own uses, but our apartment was so crammed with furniture and ornaments that we could hardly move. Things that had been packed and carted a dozen times were finally unpacked and sorted, and the Holy Roman building in Umbria re-emerged.

Venice was proving the perfect place to squander our shrinking family fortunes. We would requisition a corner table at Florian's *caffè* and sit through whole afternoons looking out over St Mark's Square, watching the flotsam and jetsam and the *haute couture* of Europe wander by. Seeing so many disparate groups struggling to complete their itineraries reminded me of my own belongings scattered like thistledown across Britain and Italy. The small castle in England from my previous marriage had been sold, and my share of its contents was gathering guano in a Norfolk barn. The hunting lodge in the extreme north of Scotland (bought for next to nothing and then abandoned) was still wailing dirges down its cracked and disused chimneys. I loved this Scottish folly, but my family disliked its isolation; so damaged dinner services, manuscripts and crates of books were stored in its lonely rooms, as well as under the beds and in the broom cupboards of my friends and relations.

My passion for accumulating bric-à-brac had been requited at the Aylsham sales, an East Anglian auction ground with rich pickings for hoarders. Every Monday there would be such a glut of lots for sale, and relatively so few bidders, that I was able to acquire endless rooms full of furniture and junk. Until I could have a palatial house to keep them in, I was comforted by these contents. One of my closest friends was a local carter, who not only moved all the truckloads of things but stored them as well. Another regular at the auctions was the Tenpenny Man, who bought all unsold lots for 10 pence. Compared to him, I was in the financial stratosphere, making a £2 bid on all furniture and 50 pence on ornaments.

Each time I moved from England to Italy, I would travel out with some of these things packed in my trunks. Over the years, I managed to move hundreds of objects of varying sizes, although in the way of furniture only chairs and folding tables could be squeezed into the trunks. Thus, in Italy, in the province of Genoa, a mere fifty-minute bus ride from the coast, I had a house full of objects, papers and beach stuff. These had all been locked up and requisitioned by the landlord, who threatened to take me to court. He was a man who thrived on quarrels and, like a character from *Bleak House*, needed the thrill of the courtroom as an antidote to life. Four years later, I was still waiting for him to see reason and give me back my things.

4

Heading down towards Tuscany, and nearer to the coast, sat 'Raguggia' – a beautiful landlocked ruin with little plumbing and no mod-cons but wonderful views. This too was still full of books and papers, linen and rugs, and a lot of skilfully mended china. At a time when we had nowhere else to live, it had been Robbie's and my first love-nest in Italy, and we had carried all the landlord's heavy chestnut furniture and our own trunks and the children's toys across a precipitous goat track that was the only access.

Circumstances and a great deal of apathy had led to our never getting round to moving out. When we left for Siena, it was largely because Allie and Iseult could not cope with the winter snows on the goat track on their daily trek to school. However, we were intending to return for another summer. But Venice intervened; and then, with no warning, we found Sant' Orsola.

Our first visit to Umbria was the last stand on the villa hunt. It was intended to confirm the hopelessness of the Holy Roman ruined castle as a summer place for us. Sometimes I would wake in the night yearning for the long pigsties to be simply pigsties, with a fabulous unseen castle beyond. There was a time when if a house had a roof I would deem it unromantic and unworthy of my attention. I'd read that the Marchesa Casati lived in a huge roofless palace in Venice, and for years I yearned to emulate her. Since then, I had lived in big houses, sheltering inside under large umbrellas, and the allure of the open sky had palled. Moving slowly, but not reluctantly, towards my middle years, I had learnt to keep one eye out for comfort, and a roofless ruin was definitely on the far side of the palings I had staked around my dream.

While workmen moved into our flat in Venice, we shifted back briefly to Siena, where a lease was still running on the dark house we had rented there. Needless to say, this house had looked like a minor treasure during the height of summer, filled with bowls of flowers, windows and doors thrown open to bees and butterflies and delicate slices of sunlight. From September to June, a pervading gloom seeped through the minuscule barred windows by day, and a film of green mould settled on everything by night. Because of the heavy atmosphere, the funereal light and a permanent fault in the wiring (which made not only all appliances but also most of the walls give off electric shocks) we called that house the Electric Chair. Legend has it that the Romans used to throw their prisoners off the sheer rock face at the edge of the small village near our house, but having tried to spend a winter there in its arctic microclimate and sinister atmosphere, I am convinced that those ancient deaths were suicides.

Setting off for Umbria from the Electric Chair seemed to bode well for our enterprise. We would have been satisfied with anything better than where we were, and it was hard to imagine many places more unappetizing. The drive to Umbria began to take on aspects of an escape. I made great preparations for it, far more, in fact, than I would make for a transatlantic trip. The road map clearly showed both Siena and Perugia (and the short distance between them) yet it struck me as essential that we set off before dawn for an eleven o'clock appointment with the Holy Roman vendor.

The Venetian reaction to our coming to Umbria to look at property had been scornful, but only with the usual scorn reserved for all things alien to the lagoon. The Sienese waiter who served us dinner on the eve of our venture was much more specific: the Umbrians were an uncivilized bunch of bandits and peasants who never salted their food, couldn't cook, and suffered from unsightly goitres. They had, he assured us, no idea of even the basic principles of architecture, and lived in huts, a prey to poverty, bears and wolves. This report was not unlike the one we had received of the Tuscans when we moved from the clement coastline of Liguria towards Siena. The bears and the wolves were an added touch, and I began to fantasize about a bear house – a Gothic room with a stone floor where a bear could hibernate during the short winters.

The journey was over almost before it had begun. By eight o'clock we were picking over the remains of a large English breakfast in the Brufani Hotel in Perugia, an establishment designed in the last century to cater for the tastes of English tourists. I grew up on a diet of Byron, Keats and Shelley; I worshipped Italy as a pilgrim might worship Mecca from afar, determined someday to go there. As a girl, I had married for the chance to live in Italy. I can hardly remember a time when I wasn't in love with the idea of it. Sitting out on the Corso Vanucci, with the pastel pink and ivory Umbrian marble warming in the morning sun, surrounded by palatial banks and offices, with grey-green hills at one end and the great Medieval Fontana Maggiore at the other, I fell in love with Umbria. But then, I fall in love with places readily. I have been in love with so many places that, like old lovers, I can no longer remember all their names.

The trip to the castle was doomed from the moment the vendor stopped his car after twenty minutes of bumping up a stony track, parked it and transferred us to the four-wheel drive of the local surveyor. A path led us through woods and fields until, fifteen laborious minutes later, we stopped by one of the few unprepossessing views of the morning.

'And this . . .' said the vendor, waving his arms towards a barely perceptible dip in the nettles around us, 'could be the amphitheatre!' On closer questioning, this suggestion proved to be the fruit of a personal fantasy.

From the outside, it was immediately clear that the photocopied photograph had, if anything, flattered the edifice. Inside, there was a thoroughly modern kitchenette with an *en suite* shower room, a small concrete hall with a massive fourteenth-century fireplace that had been ripped from an outside wall beyond it, leaving a gaping hole some four metres square. There were not only no roofs, there were no floors or ceilings beyond the modern flatlet. Where the 'fifteen-foot-wide Renaissance Imprunetta tiled staircase' was advertised, there was yet another open space with a couple of reddish traces against the wall, which could, on forensic inspection, have been terracotta.

Some hundred metres along, through hundreds of years of debris that had all but turned into arable land, there was the fabled vaulted stable. Above it, a brand-new bungalow leered down. With fractionally less undergrowth between them, the neighbourly gesture of a handshake could have been achieved without either party leaving their own home.

Edging up against the 'castle' wall, or what was left of it, there was just enough land to espalier a naturally thin tree in lieu of a garden. Wherever more than fifty pieces of stone had contrived to sit together, long wide structural cracks endeavoured to spell the word 'epicentre' across what was once the Holy Roman façade.

Meanwhile, the vendor was on automatic pilot, highlighting the potential, while using that special estate agent's alchemy to turn disaster to advantage. Thus the structure quickly became a project for a series of hi-tech kitchenettes with *en suite* minstrels' galleries and an interlocking chain of inner courtyards. These last were to cater for the bits that had already been demolished.

I have seen ruins that I would have virtually sold my soul for, but this wasn't one of them. It has been said that the stinging nettle was introduced to Britain by the Roman army as a means of conquering the cold. Roman soldiers were supposed to flagellate their naked limbs with them and in the torment forget their chills. This very Roman presence, the common stinging nettle, was growing everywhere, inside and out. I was nursing my own swollen hands on the way back to our car and its newly ruined suspension, when the diminutive local surveyor volunteered:

'Will you come and see somewhere else? It isn't far and it's a very different product.'

The vendor, who turned out to be a multiple vendor with a stake in many different hearts, then led us some twenty miles away to visit a villa on five floors.

The sight of any beautiful house or garden makes my heart miss a beat. I grew up making Sunday visits to the botanical gardens at Kew. Holidays were spent visiting the great English country houses (for a small fee and a couple of hours at a time), and Sunday evenings were spent in Clapham poring over the property advertisements in the *Sunday Times* with my mother and our mutual delusions of grandeur. We used to fantasize constantly about buying and moving into now this castle, now that. Superimposed on these childhood memories was my own dream house; as our cortège of cars turned into a drive past a triple row of venerable black cypresses, I saw the house I had been looking for all my life. It was standing like a jilted beauty still dressed in its ancient best. The abandoned façade was groaning under tons of sculpted terracotta. There was row upon row of long, graceful windows reaching down to white marble sills, there were dozens of arches, a loggia, a roof, a balcony and a cascade of wisteria.

I gleaned these impressions during my first glances. Then, though I subsequently climbed through one of the missing windows and roamed around for nearly an hour, I was so entranced that I saw little else that I could remember

9

with any clarity. There was a white marble staircase stretching up with cantilevered vertigo through four floors with neither balustrade nor banister against the sheer drop. There was a carved white marble fireplace, some ten feet high, in a blackened kitchen. There were two tractors, a combine harvester and a transport van all rusting in the downstairs hall. There were some decaying pigs' feet hanging from a wire washing-line somewhere on the third floor. There were several locked doors; I would say almost half the house was locked or barricaded away from sight. Only much later, a year later, did I notice that those locked doors were the only doors inside or out that remained on the entire villa. At the time, I was too lost in wonder to see the detail of what I knew to be our house.

Robbie and I had agreed to buy this villa, no matter what, from the moment we turned into its dusty drive. We began juggling lists of friends and family who might be willing to share the project and stretch our own pygmy capital to whatever might be the asking price of such a beauty. An hour later, I found myself in a small office in a nearby town handing over a cheque for 20 per cent of its price, in return for which I was given a sheet of lined paper with a lot of names and dates of birth on it, along with a glancing reference to the purchase of the Villa Orsola. There then followed a long discussion of terms for paying the remainder of the purchase price. My concentration here was not at its best, for I was voraciously hungry and unable to cope with the minutiae of monies that I neither had nor knew quite how to get. We were accorded six months' grace to pay the rest and I trusted that during the intervening months something would turn up to cover it.

I was instructed in the art of buying houses by Ted Hughes, our Poet Laureate, who explained to me that first I should find the house I wanted and then I should buy it, and only later worry about how to pay for it. After a couple of trial runs that led me near to but not on to the road to bankruptcy, I found this method to be almost as sound in its field as Parkinson's Law itself. The Villa Orsola was bigger than anything else I had tackled before, but then it was my dream house. The *compromesso* was duly signed, the 20 per cent deposit handed over in the form of a Eurocheque (with the usual theoretical £300 limit), and we became the new owners of an unfinished *palazzo*.

Ours was a hollow house; empty of most of the usual fittings, such as floors and doors, drains and water. All its internal decorations were verbal: the numerous versions of its history and the anecdotes surrounding its past. On our first day, we heard that the Villa Orsola had been built entirely in the seventeenth, eighteenth and nineteenth centuries, and that it had been built for a famous architect, a gambler, a nobleman, a general, a Frenchman, a Greek, a German, and so on through all the nations and professions. No two stories agreed, and yet everyone seemed to have a tale about '*il palazzo*'. What did emerge was that the seemingly abandoned shell at the edge of the village was somehow very close to its centre, drawing generation after generation into its bare rooms with a quality that lay somewhere between magnetism and magic.

It was between false walls built in the *palazzo* that the village grain had been hidden from the Germans during the last war. It was on the lumpy rubble outside it that the old men had played football when they were lads, before the new football pitch was built. School outings were organized under its decaying arches; village fêtes took place in its halls; there were dances, balls and dates. The Villa Orsola had never really been lived in, but countless children had been conceived there against its acres of virgin plaster-work.

Later that evening, we headed back to Siena in a haze of

good fortune. We had a roll of film to be developed, but meanwhile we had to make do with our memories of the villa. With the excitement and the strain of being raced through the *compromesso* document with all its double standards of sale, I had achieved a new personal best in doziness. The asking price had been so low that it had seemed ungracious to nitpick about the details, so I had daydreamed as they slipped by. As we rolled down the motorway, I asked Robbie to tell me again the name of the hamlet we had just bought our way into, and its nearby village, because I had somehow forgotten both these things. Robbie had not forgotten – with his faltering grip of Italian he had never heard them in the first place, but had assumed that I would know, as I was the linguist and the practical one. So we found ourselves cruising along the *autostrada*, either the victims of a confidence trick or the owners of a nameless pile of exquisitely decorated masonry just outside a village that we could neither of us find again, even on a map.

Chapter 2

Illness and accident took their toll on the family, swallowing up the best part of a year. So it was not until the spring of 1989 that I found myself travelling from Venice to Umbria to show my two children the place where they were to live. The eldest, known as the child Iseult, was visibly outgrowing her title. At fifteen she had modelled, albeit briefly, in both London and Paris. Her life was full of wonderful offers which, though none materialized, gave her an aura of glamour among her peers, who delighted in discussing her potential stardom, bandying the names of the rich and famous as though they were all old and dear friends. The child's social life was so hectic that it made mine look like the feeble meanderings of a geriatric. Addicted as she was to the long-distance use of the telephone, I was a little apprehensive about taking her to a villa that not only had no phone, but no light, water, windows or doors, not to mention a serious gap in the roof.

I was even more worried about the effect this abandoned building site might have on her six-year-old brother, Allie, who had been indoctrinated by the nuns of San Giuseppe into a world of perfect order. In Venice, a scuff on his outdoor shoes or a wrinkle in his broad white collar or flowing black smock meant being sent home for the day. His homework was written in exercise books filled with tiny squares where full stops and commas were raised a regulation number of millimetres from their usual place. To lose this precision was a frequent cause of tears.

I dreaded showing them the discomfort that lay before us if we were ever to make the villa habitable. I had been down there with Robbie some weeks before to sign the final documents and hand over the last of the monies, and it was only then that we realized what a huge gap there was between the dream house we had first seen and its practical completion. Neither of us had noticed quite how much was missing until then. Now Robbie was nursing his terminally ill father in Scotland, and it was up to me to start the restoration of the villa. I could think of no way of attacking a problem of such size without somehow camping there. It followed that the children would have to forgo their usual summer by the sea and camp with me.

Considering that I have spent no small fraction of my life on trains, I should be better informed about the various lines, but alas this is not so. A friend assured me that Cortona was the nearest station to our new house, and it was to Cortona–Camucia that we were bound. Days designed for children's treats are usually doomed to failure, and this one was no exception. The lack of taxis was our first disappointment, the lack of refreshment another. After nearly an hour of wheedling, a battered estate car came bumping down the hot dusty hill towards us. Although we had planned only a two-day trip, our luggage would have sufficed for a two-month safari. Our cases were duly taken to a very pleasant hotel in the centre of Cortona, and our driver was persuaded to wait for us while we ate lunch and then take us on to Città di Castello.

We set off for Umbria on a back road across the mountains that our driver claimed to know well. An hour later, after crawling round innumerable vertiginous curves, we left our pasta *parpardella* with hare and parsley by the roadside, and only two hours later did we arrive at the door of the local *geometra*'s office. There was no need to collect keys: there were no doors. We had decided to get the taxi driver to drop us at the villa, having asked the *geometra* to pick us up two hours later, thus giving ourselves some time there on our own.

I had told the child Iseult about the Marchesa Casati's roofless palace in Venice and how she had thrown great parties and been the outrageous leader of fashion, by way of romanticizing the sixty-foot stretch of roof that was missing at Sant' Orsola, and the gaping split where the two parts of the villa, one eighteenth- and one nineteenth-century, had never been fully joined. I had told Allie that he could have his own football pitch where he could play to his heart's content without the old ladies of Venice coming out and chiding him and his friends away. In the forty minutes it took to ride on from Città di Castello to Sant' Orsola I passed from persuasion to bribery and then to silence, regretting for the first time having embarked on this venture.

On arrival, it was the taxi driver who was most distressed by the sight of the family ruin. He sat down on the bonnet of his car for some minutes, shaking his head and swearing. Then he offered to drive us back to the safety of Cortona for free rather than leave us in such a desolate shell. The child's first reaction to the place was one of disappointment. Used to the truly palatial proportions of Venetian buildings, she accused me of having called the villa huge, whereas really, she said, it wasn't. Meanwhile, Allie found the whole house enchanting and could find no fault with any of it, and took it upon himself to walk his big sister around again to show her its potential. They found a cardboard box with six new-born kittens in it on the third floor. Then, outside, Allie ran a race and fell off the edge of a terraced field and landed on his head.

For the last half-hour of our visit, I walked Iseult around the heaps of rubble that would one day be our garden. I showed her where the knot garden would be, where there would be pergolas, a rose garden, a wisteria avenue, lily ponds and shrubberies. She listened with the kindly, patient face of an asylum nurse. Although she clearly thought my plans for the garden were unattainable nonsense, walking around the outside of the house had given her some sense of its actual size, and she began to get excited at the thought of once more living in a big house. For all but the last four years of her life we had lived in roomy houses, and she often pined for space. Following those other big houses there had been trunks and trains and a lot of squatting in what was to her eye squalid (and to mine, picturesque) pensions. Here at least was a chance to spread out, to entertain her friends, and to play her ghetto-blaster as loud as she liked.

By five o'clock the hard part of the day was supposed to be over. The *geometra* picked us up as planned, took us into Città di Castello and treated us to ice-creams. We sat in the window of a double-fronted *caffè* looking out across the square to a taxi rank. The *geometra* had an appointment (as *geometras* always do, living their lives like hamsters on a wheel), but he offered to drop us somewhere if we needed. We were happy with our ice-creams and secure in the knowledge of the waiting taxis, so we parted.

Within minutes it started to rain. A great grey curtain was arbitrarily pulled over the afternoon. The square was cleared as if by a bomb scare and a chill began to settle all around us. The two purring taxis had both disappeared, and although we waited and waited, they failed to turn up again. We combed through the telephone directory for taxi numbers and spoke to a great many wives and sisters. There were only two cabs in Città di Castello itself, and one had gone to Rome and the other to a wedding outside

Florence. Neither of them would be back that night. The driver from Cortona, who was very much a last resort with his self-imposed speed limit of eight kilometres per hour, had gone. Everyone had gone, it seemed, and was having a good time.

In true party spirit, we ordered a mass of custard-cream doughnuts and yet more ice-cream. The waitress brought them very gracefully to our table and then asked us to eat them quickly as she was about to close. We decided to cut our losses and give up the idea of returning to Cortona, and set out in search of a hotel to shelter from the rain and make the most of the rest of the evening. Both Iseult and Allie were feeling sick. A random sampling revealed that 70 per cent of the population didn't know if there was a hotel in town, but at least half of these knew there used to be one and could direct you to its gutted shell. Another 10 per cent could point you towards a *pensione* closed for the winter which would not reopen till June. Another 10 per cent seemed to find the whole question disturbing and improper and shied away from answering at all except to point out that Allie would catch cold. Then there were the statutory men who had, or had not, received their handsome lessons with the appropriate pouts and poses, and who didn't know of a hotel, as such, but would be only too glad to reopen their offices and be as entertaining as only they knew how. Lastly, there was a handful of people who spoke of a certain Hotel America as though it were a distant continent beyond the damp comfort of the medieval city wall. This latter group divided into those who sent us off in the direction of the cathedral and the public garden, and those who sent us in the opposite direction, down the hilly main street past all the closed shops and bars.

It was there, pacing the stone-flagged streets of Città di Castello, that the Villa Orsola, by default, first came to feel like home. The temperature had plummeted as the evening advanced, and the rain had become torrential. Having set out in warm sunshine for an afternoon's jaunt, we none of us had coats, and I was wearing rope-soled espadrilles. Squelching up and down those ancient streets between the rows of shuttered windows, we longed for the warmth of a log fire and somewhere to sit. We all wished that we had stayed and camped at the Villa Orsola, which was our own, instead of having to try our luck in the dark in this small city whose grandeur offered no comfort.

That night we slept badly, all sharing a damp bed in the suburbs. Then we collected our luggage from the hotel in Cortona and returned to Venice to plan a new campaign that would include occupying the villa and staying there until it became fit to live in. We decided to return as soon as possible, armed with as many basic essentials as we could carry between us (I don't drive), and to camp in what would one day be the big kitchen on the first floor. Allie would follow us two weeks later with the two Irish au pairs, when the villa had been equipped with running water, sanitation and some slightly safer floors, at ground level at least.

Both the Irish au pairs had seen a rather too flattering photograph of the best façade of the villa, but neither knew of the sorry state that it was reduced to. I hadn't dared tell them, for fear they would flee. I had warned them that there was an enormous amount of building work to be done, but I suspected that the term 'enormous' did not adequately describe the task ahead.

Chapter 3

We packed and repacked our suitcases at least a dozen times. We had two foam beach mats, a ghetto-blaster and a blanket; these took up most of the space. I twice went through the familiar ritual of removing sections of Iseult's wardrobe and multitudinous bottles from the bathroom cabinet from the luggage and refilling it with plates, cups, coats and tools. Twice was not enough. When our taxi finally pulled into the wrecked grounds of the Villa Orsola, having taken the mountain road from the supposedly neighbouring Arezzo at five kilometres per hour, I was too car-sick to check anything. The taxi driver left, a wealthier but worried man. It was a warm, sunny afternoon and dandelions and speedwells were growing in the clipped meadow in front of the house. As we unpacked, more and more of the luggage seemed to consist of my daughter's clothes, shoes, boots and facepacks.

I thought I had travelled to Umbria prepared for most contingencies, arming us with everything from firelighters to groundsheets, thermal rugs, power torches and dozens of useful miscellanies designed to cushion our first few days and weeks of camping in our country house. But the child Iseult had a supremely impractical mind and a ruthless dedication to the world of her fantasies and the pursuit of her already considerable beauty. She had a naturally curious and trusting nature which not only made her endlessly sociable but spilled over into gullibility when it came to anything to do with her complexion, her figure or her personal attire. No substance had ever been deemed too recherché to use on her hair or skin so long as it came recommended by a magazine or a friend.

So, where the average facepack might come in the form of a small sachet which would slip into the side pocket of a suitcase, the child's facepacks consisted of a collection of kilner jars filled with varying degrees of sludge and slime: concoctions of food, mud and herbs that were so far past their sell-by dates that they had begun to form pondlife. In Venezuela, where she was born and spent her formative years, it is the practice to leave little bowls of decaying washing suds on every sill and under every piece of furniture. Whether or not this addiction to multiple ferments is a national trait, it is one I have lived with for nearly two decades without getting any nearer to liking. In Umbria, as I unpacked our bags on the stone slabs around the kitchen fireplace, it was the jars of gunge that I found particularly galling. The lack of most of what might have been useful, and some of what I considered essential, for our comfort and even survival was hard to accept. The three Japanese kimonos, two pairs of Edwardian riding boots, five pairs of evening shoes, the tea gowns, beaded dresses, evening dresses and the green velvet cape that had replaced them seemed superfluous to either of our needs; but the pots of stagnating oatmeal, cucumber juice and eggs, and the fetid blobs of camomile, cabbage and honey, were the poorest substitute for our utensils I could think of.

The child was entirely unrepentant, saving her sorrow for the sorry state of her concoctions. This was the beginning of our new life. This was the time we had always dreamed of; an end to our wanderings with a place of our own on our own terms at last. 'Surely,' she asked me, 'we are not going to fall out at such a crucial time and over such a trivial matter?' Wrapped in her silken nightdresses, the tape deck with its eight jumbo batteries and a collection of cassettes had remained intact, and we swept the soot, cobwebs and rubble out of the kitchen to the strains of Puccini alternating with blasts of Van Morrison.

After shifting a few clouds of dust from one side of the room to the other with a bundle of twigs, the child climbed down completely, disarming me with her remorse. She was sorry, she would make amends, she would make a list of all that we needed and somehow we would procure it the next day.

'You just relax, sit on the suitcase, everything'll be fine here, you'll see.'

She sat in the window, in the space where shutters and glass and frame should have been, with the massive stone fireplace on her right, and hill slopes of oakwoods rising up outside to her left, chewing a pencil and making a list. It began with our missing luggage: a dustpan and brush, firelighters, more matches, a torch, washing-up liquid, a frying pan, first-aid kit, waterproof squares, a blanket. Then it moved on to food stuffs, and from what we could eat to what she could put on her face. This is a family of lists, they act as a palliative, a universal balm.

Beyond the window, bats began to swoop, circling through the streams of early evening air. The temperature dropped suddenly and the cool breeze brought in eddies of woodland scents: the last of the blackthorn and the first of the hawthorn and broom, all filtered through cypress resin. The child and I went back out into the scrubland around the villa and gathered bundles of broom twigs as light as straw. Then we rooted around among the poppies and dandelions for larger twigs, making up bundles to add to the long sticks from a mossy woodpile we had found stacked conveniently behind the house. These oak sticks, each as thick as my arm, were carefully sawn into five-foot lengths, which rendered them singularly unwieldy. We made our first blaze from them (without firelighters) in the fireplace in the big kitchen, with its high ceiling, its eight metres square of stone floor, its old stone sink in one corner, its long windows on two sides, and its door. This chestnut door was one of the five doors in the house. This kitchen, together with two adjoining rooms on the first floor, had been used as a caretaker's flat over the last hundred years. The ceiling and walls were steeped in smoke, but the beautiful carved white marble fireplace that we had seen (and bought), with its grimy crests and pillars, had been stolen some months earlier. A stone placebo had been erected in its place by the penitent vendors. I subsequently discovered that ripping historical fireplaces out of their masonry is almost as popular a sport here as shooting songbirds.

As the sunny afternoon turned into an increasingly chilly evening, I climbed under the new stone mantel and tried to forget my rancour at this theft. There was so little in the villa that it seemed doubly sad to lose this one treasure, gutted in its turn from a Savoyard palace somewhere, as its crests had testified.

We ate pasta cooked over the open fire. Our one bottle of still water had been replaced by a luscious housecoat, so we used our fizzy water and ate fizzy pasta which Iseult loyally claimed to like. When I drained the hot gassy water into the sink, we discovered that not only did it have no water, but it was not even connected to the most rudimentary drain, and a thick steaming paste ran over the kitchen floor. The dregs of its effervescence threatened our own, edging towards us and our island of beach mats.

We stoked up the fire with the long pieces of oak sapling and retired to our bed. There was nothing to be done about the approaching pasta paste and nothing to be done inside our barricaded kitchen. In the surrounding twilight, there were night noises. A screech owl seemed to have lost both its mate and its senses somewhere very near to our open windows. Across the hills and along the valley, a series of dogs were yelping and yapping, exchanging semi-hysterical canine greetings, while a chorus of crickets kept up a steady invasion of the silence. Trees sighed, timbers creaked, foxes shrieked, flayed shutters slammed, and our imaginations ran away with us. By the fire- and candlelight, the sounds multiplied until it seemed the only refuge was sleep.

Our mattresses, so comfortable on a Venetian beach, seemed absurdly thin when laid on bare stone, but we slept despite them, and both woke aching and freezing after what seemed like a long hard night, only to find that it was actually half-past ten and the night had not yet begun. Every time the oak sticks burnt through, the fire died down to a handful of charcoal. We played cards, slamming down the Neapolitan faces with all the energy we could muster in the hope of exorcising the uncanny noises around us and keeping the mosquitoes at bay.

When the card games flagged, we talked and drank fizzy tea. We told ourselves how pretty the loggia would look in the morning, its tall brick pillars crested with terracotta laced with a trellis of wisteria. We would eat our breakfast there, disregarding the holes that fell through to the cellar; we would find the sound bits of the floor and start some of the hundreds of chores that were now on our lists. For the L-shaped loggia we had:

1. Remove bedsprings, bicycles, bits of cars, etc., and make pile.
2. Remove broken glass.
3. Gather up all bits of wood, chairs, butterchurn, etc., and burn.
4. Mark out weak bits of floor with buoys, like lagoon.

5 Remove cobwebs, sweep.
6 Kill scorpions.
7 Find pots or tins and collect ferns.
6 Construct table and chairs.
7 Make lovely.
8 Find hammocks and hang them.
9 Mend floor, reinforce, relay, etc.
10 Light.
11 Some statues, wall, fountain, etc.

'Etcetera' was our big word, it allowed us to roam through the villa, restoring it in our imaginations. The lists lengthened, and the woodpile shrank. We slept in snatches regulated by our waning furnace. We were soon very tired and cold. The voracious fireplace didn't seem to want saplings, it cried out for trees. Once the kindling was finished, it gave only a grudging heat.

Neither of us felt brave enough to venture past our barricaded door to replenish our wood from the stack outside. The discordant symphony of sounds and cries continued throughout the night. We wrapped ourselves in all the child's finery and waited for morning. The sun rose at six, climbing over the hills with a pale glow, picking out the patches of wild cherry blossom in the woods.

As we gathered twigs from the bushes of broom that circled the property, the sweet scent of its first flowers sitting on the morning air, the fears of the night vanished and seemed absurd. We relit the fire and warmed ourselves as the piles of dead broom twigs went up the chimney in hundreds of sparks like primitive roman candles. House-martins swooped about the windowsills carrying mud and fluff to their nests, while a multitude of brightly coloured finches darted in the branches of the cypress trees. Somewhere in the fields beyond them a flock of sheep stirred with their bells.

The menacing cries of the previous night had faded or been transformed into recognizable country noises. We stayed in the kitchen, basking in the morning sun and sleeping our first proper sleep, incorporating all the sounds pleasantly into our slumber. By seven o'clock, these sounds had become articulate Italian male voices directly outside our door. Another voice called from outside, 'O, Imolo!' and the men retreated to carry out a shouting match through the gaping masonry.

This was the core of our workforce, of whom Imolo was the master mason. I didn't know then that I would be spending as much time with him as with my own family. His strange name echoed through the neighbourhood like a battle cry as we made ourselves as presentable as we could in our dishevelled state. The child Iseult rose to the occasion by donning a black-velvet tea gown and evening gloves to the elbow. Between us, we managed to terrify the workforce by emerging from what they thought to be an empty ruin.

Imolo took the matter in hand, explaining politely to us that after decades of having been a free-for-all, the villa had now become private property and the owners were due to arrive any day, any minute. As he spoke, he peered around anxiously to see who else we had concealed on his surrogate territory. We had packed away our beach mats and scant bedding and there was nothing left of our night's inhabitation but the river of congealed slime on the floor, which he eyed with distaste and suspicion. I took it as a mark of his extreme hospitality that, despite our apparent intrusion, he offered to accompany us to his house for coffee and biscuits with his wife before seeing us on our way.

'It's very near,' he assured us. 'We start working here today, and the owners won't want to find you here.'

'I *am* the owner,' I told him.

Imolo's piercing blue eyes smiled while two of his colleagues who were propping each other up in the door jamb swallowed their laughter into a strangled duet of 'Eh, *sì*, eh!'

'Yes,' I said as briskly as it would come, 'I am the owner who has bought the villa, and this is my daughter, Iseult.'

The three men looked from one of us to the other, eyeing up the child with lascivious appraisal and then turning back to me.

'*Parla italiano?*' Imolo asked me.

'But we are speaking Italian.'

'Yes,' he said doubtfully, 'but we're not talking any sense. You see, I've spoken to the *geometra* and the vendor, and I know that the new owners are a middle-aged couple and very distinguished. No one said anything about two girls.'

'I am not a girl,' I insisted, 'I'm a *signora*. There may have been some exaggeration about the distinction, but my husband and I have bought this villa and now we are moving in.'

Imolo eyed the gluey pasta sludge sadly and then rummaged through his pockets in search of a cigarette. The one he found emerged from a crushed and dusty packet.

'I am the *signora*, I'm just a bit tired,' I insisted lamely, and the child chipped in to verify my claim. I have always had an unnaturally quiet voice; a childish voice and a childlike face. As the years accumulate around me, the latter has been the cause of much gratifying flattery, but the former has always been a nuisance. When I lived in Venezuela and managed a sugar plantation, strangers never believed that it was I who was the boss. More recently, during the years of my literary career, unless I take pains to alter my voice on the telephone, callers still ask me to call my mummy so that they can speak to me.

'Let's go and call the *geometra*, if you like. I know him, and he can tell you that we are who we say.'

Imolo laughed; then he apologized and grappled my elbow for a few seconds.

'You've surprised us. Welcome to Sant' Orsola. Life is a strange thing. Where do you start on something like this?' he said, waving his cigarette stub above his head. 'And how come you speak Italian already if you've only just arrived?'

I explained that we had been living in Venice and Siena. In time-honoured fashion he completely ignored the reference to Siena and told me and his mates, '*Venezia é bella*, but nowhere is as beautiful as Sant' Orsola.' He seemed much sobered by the thought and shook himself out of his reverie by delivering a playful punch to Iseult's stomach. Then he made a last fleeting inspection of the corners of the room for signs, I suppose, of my husband and asked slyly, 'And your husband?'

'He's not here yet. He's coming later.'

Imolo smiled in an infuriatingly knowing way, as though the absence of Robbie had rendered my story absurd, and took his leave.

Chapter 4

As soon as they were safely away, sweeping and shouting and tipping clouds of dust and lumps of rubble out of the top-floor windows, the child and I made our way down to the village. We followed the dusty track around its twists and turns between ditches clogged with bulrushes turned to down by nesting birds. On either side, the fields were being made ready for tobacco planting. Piles of pig manure were being tilled into the furrows. Although we were nominally going out for a wash, some breakfast and to buy supplies, the child had taken this trip to be her début into what she hoped would be a busy social life. Despite the morning sun which had banished all traces of the previous night's cold, she set out in full regalia, complete with her green velvet cloak. Long before we had covered the mile of track encrusted with sharp chips of stone, her high-heeled satin shoes were shredded.

What we had taken to be a small bar at the end of our road was closed and battened. We sat for a moment in a ditch of horse's-tail weed and half-burnt litter under the shade of a walnut tree while we struggled to overcome our disappointment. A curious tractor driver paused in his labours, drove his tractor almost up to our feet and asked both who we were and whether he could be of any assistance. The weathered skin of a farmer was stretched over his fair Etruscan features, and his reddish blond hair was carefully cut in the style of a mushroom cap.

'We're looking for a bar.'

'No problem,' he said, and pointed towards a stone shack clinging to the side of the hill behind us. 'Call out for Regina and you'll be served. I'd come with you, but I'm working. I'll meet you there later if you like.'

Regina answered our call as though we had long been patrons of her camouflaged establishment. She emerged from a dark wine cellar on the ground floor, muttering something to a chicken she was holding in her left hand by its feet. When we asked for *cappuccino*, she looked moment-arily nonplussed. After a few seconds of deliberation, she casually knocked the chicken against a petrol pump beside us, tucked it under her arm to still its shuddering death throes and made her way up some stone steps to the first floor. Ten minutes later, she re-emerged with an enamel tray, two cups of *cappuccino* and a large bundle of keys.

The bar itself was a small dark room with a composite marble floor and a large counter. Four tables set with chairs were spaced forlornly around it. Behind the counter, and a stone sink, small bottles of pear juice were stacked in pyramids. At either end of the counter, cellophane bags of pistachios and melon seeds were arranged on a spike. The rest of the bar consisted of a collection of large, unlabelled bottles of cloudy yellow and black wine and several crates of fizzy orangeade.

Regina came to join us as we drank our tepid coffee, glad, she said, of the break. Her sleeves were rolled up to reveal amazingly powerful biceps. Her fingers drummed restlessly on the Formica table-top. She was encouragingly friendly, explaining the geography of the village to us, asking few questions and offering not only information but a gift of fresh eggs and a mortadella sandwich, which she disappeared out to buy for Iseult. She added to the geography a little social history, all interspersed with the loud clearing of her blocked nasal passages. Catching a look of surprise on the child's face the first time she did this, she explained that she suffered from chronic sinusitis.

'I have taken the mud inhalations at Fontecchio,' she told us, 'but it means getting up at five and getting into Castello, and with seven children and one of them wrong in the head and all these chickens to be plucked and gutted, I just can't keep up with my appointments.'

We were joined by Carlo, who wandered in and stood hovering behind his mother, dangling the dripping dead chicken by its legs. Regina introduced us to her son, adding fondly, 'He's the one who's not right in the head.'

Carlo was tall and thin with dark curls and a permanent shy grin. He walked with his head jutting slightly forward. Most Italian men publicly touch their genitals at regular intervals, as though to check that they are still there. Carlo seemed to have been born with a premonition of loss, as one hand was permanently clamped on his trousers, checking and touching. Regina's hands were never still either. When she finished drumming, she grabbed the dead chicken and began to pluck it over the floor with real dexterity. Having thus stripped the thin, yellow-skinned bird, she disembowelled it, without pausing in her conversation.

We located the bathroom, a cubicle beyond the bar room, and took it in turns to slip away and wash in the tiny basin. We also found that what had at first seemed such an ill-equipped bar was actually full of promise: there was a payphone. I called Robbie in Scotland where he was nursing his father and told him how well we were coping, and I called the Irish au pairs in Venice to check on Allie. He was at school.

'Who were you calling?' Regina asked me.
'My husband.'

'Why would you call your husband?'

'He's a long way away.'

'*Bé!* What luck, mine never is! He'll be in in a minute, snouting out the wine.' On cue, a short, stout, purple-faced man lurched through the door and grinned with the same sheepish grin as his damaged son.

'*Buon dì,*' he announced and turned in a practised movement towards the counter. Regina thrust the gutted chicken at the child Iseult and sprang up from her seat. Her husband was quicker, and was already behind the counter and tipping a bottle of wine unceremoniously down his throat. Regina took the bottle and cuffed him around his purple-veined head. No words were exchanged and he drifted out and back into the sunshine, shaking his head.

Cleaner and wiser, we followed him out into the sun, directed by Regina to where the several shops of the village were concealed. From a bird-like widow whose head hardly reached her cluttered counter, we purchased a mattress, some sheets, three floral blankets and a checked tablecloth. Had we been so disposed, we could have bought almost anything in the way of soft furnishings. Her shop also had a larger range of men's trousers than most major department stores, hundreds of pairs of stockings, entire racks of aprons, and stacks from floor to ceiling of navy cardigans.

By the time we reached the mattress emporium, in a row of stone houses at the centre of the village, we realized that word had preceded us. The word was that we had moved into the *palazzo*, that we were camping there, living without water, and without any men. Despite this tarnish to our respectability (or perhaps because of it) we were treated with the utmost gentleness. After buying our mattress and arranging for it to be delivered to the house, we were invited into the shopkeeper's kitchen to take coffee. The best Limoges coffee cups were taken out of the dresser and coffee laced with potent *mistrà* was placed before us on an immaculate tray of biscuits and sweatmeats, set down on a pristine chestnut table in a kitchen so clean it looked unused. I drank both my coffee and the child's and then we rose to leave. Our frail bird-like hostess urged us to return soon. 'And if you need other things, anything, please ask me . . . my husband died last summer. I'm quite lost without him, but if you have a moment . . . I'm always here.'

We hadn't bargained on buying a mattress so soon, certainly not one of such fine quality and costing so much. We would have comfort, but we suddenly didn't have any cash. At the next shop, which was *the* shop, the biggest and most widely used for food, drink and general hardware, we decided that we would have to buy so much that it would be all right to pay by cheque. We spent over an hour selecting basic china, jugs, funnels, brooms, mops, pots and pans, water, fruit, bread, cheese and chocolate. When our turn came in the queue, each item was slowly checked and then the whole recounted, the total gone over backwards and forwards, and then the bill was finally presented. I made out a cheque from the Banca Nazionale di Lavoro in Venice. The shopkeeper looked at my cheque as though it alarmed her, then tentatively she picked it up and handed it to her brother, who shook his head with a hint of real tragedy as he explained that they could not accept foreign cheques in their village shop.

'It isn't foreign, it's Venetian – Italian,' I protested.

'Well, that's pretty foreign.'

The cheque was then put up for general inspection and other shoppers were asked to examine it. There was a con-sensus of '*mai visto*' – never having seen such a thing before. Its grey-blue markings were admired by some but were not enough to convince anyone that here was a perfectly good cheque. Since the banks were already shutting in the nearest town, we had no choice but to set our purchases aside for the following day and take only the most meagre rations to tide us over our second night in Sant' Orsola.

On day three, we telephoned for a taxi, went to town, cashed money and bought not only food but more gaudy tools and a dozen crates of drinking water.

The child and I came to know the village via the workmen and Regina's bar. Day after day we trudged up and down from the villa to the village. We rarely took the lifts we were offered since our position on the edge of the village looked so bizarre and was increasingly so disturbing to the local people that we could think only of brazening it out and pretending that we enjoyed the hardship of our life there. Each day I would call Robbie and Allie on the payphone. Robbie advised me on what should be done on the house, while Allie was desperate to skip the end of his Venetian school term and join us in our life of relative deprivation. The more I described its difficulties, the more he wanted to drop everything and come. The Irish au pairs had become known as the Beauties: each hurried conversation with Allie would end with a caution, to be sure not to tell the Beauties how tough it was here, as they wouldn't come if they knew.

From day four, a mechanical digger was churning up what I laughingly called the garden, laying drains, water pipes and electricity cables. On day five, it managed to rupture the water supply to the entire neighbourhood. A delegation of distressed farmers and housewives came up to the villa to remonstrate. They seemed to know the digger man well and took his accident in good heart. To placate them, Imolo gave them a tour of the derelict husk of our house, explaining to them the minutiae of the work he had embarked on on the ground floor. He tracked me down and introduced me to all of them with a: 'This is Giovanni, you've just cut off his water across the valley,' and, 'This is Maria del Gallo, she's your next-door neighbour across the vineyard, you've just left her without any water either.'

In Venice, every one of our neighbours had had water and gas pipes running through our apartment and rights of way to inspect them. In Umbria, our neighbours' pipes ran invisibly through our land like a hidden maze of veins and arteries. It became a regular feature of the digger man's work to sever some of these pipes.

After the first few days of lugging water up the hill in clear plastic bottles bought at the local shop, there came water via a yellow plastic hosepipe which filled a large wine barrel three times a week. This hosepipe was dragged down to our nearest neighbour across the pitted moonscape behind our house, through a patch of nettles and thistles, then downhill across a vineyard and on to an outside tap at the Signora Maria's farmhouse.

The water arrived with a great deal of excitement and general instructions. As the barrel filled, the cement sediment rose and instantly clouded the new water. After the workmen left, every evening this vat became our bath. We took it in turns to immerse ourselves in the rather unpleasantly grey water, diligently scrubbing the worst of the cement dust off our parched skins with a bar of almond soap. One evening Imolo returned to get a tool from his box and caught me in his tub. Iseult warned me, but not in time for me to get out, so I sank down until only my eyes were visible over the top of the tall barrel while Imolo tried to persuade me to desist from bathing in such unsavoury sludge.

'That's not good for your skin, you know, it's not advisable to wash there, and it's dirty. It's for washing tools in, and for mixing cement.'

We made a show of having abandoned Imolo's barrel, but secretly we continued to bathe there every day. The minuscule washroom at Regina's bar was all very well for hair, teeth and faces, but the days were consistently hot and the gathering dust from the building work had a way of burrowing

34

that made even offending Imolo worth risking if it were only possible to rinse some of the patina of cement away.

The child Iseult said that just looking at Imolo moved her to tears, such was the aura of sorrow that he carried in his eyes. The child was moved to tears by many things, from advertisements to films, magazines, photographs and stray dogs, but in Imolo's case, I agreed with her, and added this power to move me to my already growing cult of Imolo. We had grown to worship him. The thought of displeasing him seemed synonymous with never making our house habitable, never clearing the alleyway of the sacks of cement and never being able to fathom the mysteries of our environment. He was our saviour and our guide. He must have had a very strange impression of our family, in those early days. He told me later that our living conditions were so bad, he would not have inflicted them on a dog. In his generous way, he turned a blind eye to the various strains of madness that he detected in our clan. Eventually, though, unable to bear the prospect of our bathing any longer in the building slops, he accelerated our plumbing installations while simultaneously urging us to relinquish the barrel and turn to the spring water and the lake.

'What lake?' I asked him, thinking of the distant shores of Lake Trasimeno.

'Giovanni's lake . . . down there,' he said, pointing into a cluster of oaks and elms beyond the barrier of our own thick cypresses.

On closer inspection, we found that there was indeed a small lake, entirely screened by trees. In winter it was visible from our house and the track, but in summer it was hidden. Everyone knew it was there, and everyone wondered why we didn't make use of it during those first days of heat and dust. It was assumed to be another of our harmless eccentricities that we preferred a barrel.

The road to the lake began as the road to Regina's bar and the village, past three stone houses and their rambling outhouses, a ruined twelfth-century tower and a small disused chapel. Together with our house, this was the hamlet of old Sant' Orsola, a fraction of the size of the main village. Numerous other scions were affiliated to old Sant' Orsola, but being more scattered, they gravitated to the huddle on the turn of the road below our villa only on feast days.

A hundred metres further downhill, there was a small shrine to the Madonnina del campo. Doubling back on the curve of a barely perceptible track through a meadow, a row of acacia and hazel trees bowed over an almost non-existent stream. We followed this trickle of water along what seemed to be an unbroken line of vegetation until we discovered a narrow gap hedged with brambles and black-thorn and a plank bridge made out of a thick rotting slab of chestnut. Between yet another screen of sheltering elms and a small sloping vineyard we found Giovanni's lake.

It was no bigger than what would one day be our ballroom, but it was fed by a hill spring and the water was pure and cold. Looking back, there were moments of fear, farce, happiness and frustration, and there were a few moments of sheer bliss. Giovanni's lake was one of those moments: a plunge into utter luxury, the icy luxury of clean unrationed water.

To our own relief at finding fresh water was added Imolo's.

'I promise you, we didn't know it was there. Do you think we'd wash in your dregs from choice?'

'Well, who am I to judge a foreigner? I was worried. We talked about it and decided not to interfere, but I think a few people are going to feel more at their ease with you when they find out you didn't know about the lake.'

'So here we are, different but not dirty.'

Imolo smiled and went on his way, continuing to trans-late our actions for the benefit of his tribe.

Chapter 5

The villa fell quite naturally into apartments. This is typical of Italian villas, built to house extended families and their workforce. So the newer, nineteenth-century rooms at the front of the house would have been designed for the owner and his family, perhaps with an apartment for grandparents, aunts, and eventually grown-up children with their families. The older, eighteenth-century part at the back would have been destined for the peasant workers, the *contadini* who would not only run the house, but also farm the land.

Unlike so many English Victorian country houses with their cramped servants' quarters and their strict divisions between family and service, upstairs, downstairs, Italian architecture was far more democratic. The families sometimes had their own kitchens, but certain areas were communal. Much of the ground floor was used as agricultural store rooms.

When we started to restore, or rather finish, the villa, we decided to keep it exactly as it would have been had the owner and architect, Giovan Battista Nicasi, not died before its completion. The only structural alterations would be to remove the accumulated disfigurements, introduced over the best part of a century, to the inside and the façade which had been intended to turn the elegant villa into an indoor farm. By moulding our needs to the original existing shapes, we would be left not so much with a large house as with a series of flats.

The plan was to ensconce the Irish Beauties and Allie in the first ground-floor flat as soon as it was ready. The one we planned to build next to it was still a derelict agricultural store. On the first floor, in the older half of the house, there was the old custodian's flat, consisting of the big kitchen and two bedrooms. In the newer half, there was a suite of six high-ceilinged, airy rooms with a long corridor joining them to the rear of the villa. This corridor ran into the stairwell at either end, giving the house a maze-like quality, compounding space and the opportunity to get lost in it.

The west end of the villa was a vast galleried ballroom or salon, the restoration of which seemed so daunting that it remained a shell and a project only in our imaginations, as it probably will for many years to come (if not indefinitely).

Upstairs again, either by the precipitous main staircase, or via the back stairs, there was another flat, which would one day be turned over to Allie and Iseult. This was also derelict, but more walled-in and divided up than the ballroom, and therefore was more feasibly a home. There was less chicken wire, fewer sinister iron hooks gaping out of the wrecked ceilings and fewer holes in the floor.

Turning on the wide inner circuit of the corridor and stairs, there was then an identical suite of rooms to those on the first floor. Only the master bedroom, or the room that was reputedly designed to be such, was different. Two of its four windows gaped low enough to be french windows, and skirting them was an L-shaped balustraded balcony in ornate terracotta. This, Imolo assured us, had been designed so that Giovan Battista Nicasi, the architect, could survey the valley and the lands that he owned away to the horizon in two directions. The patchwork of vine-yards, fields and woods that stretched up towards the hill of Muccignano were his, just as the bands of low-lying rich soil along the river-bed were his, and the valley rising up from it on either side.

'Giovan Battista Nicasi,' Imolo told us confidently, 'was mad.' Apparently he had built the entire villa up to the second floor and then demolished it and turned it around so as to get this particular view from his bedroom.

'When the villa was built, there was no water in the vicinity to use for building, to mix the cement and plaster. Giovan Battista Nicasi didn't care. He offered all the *contadini* a barrel of wine in return for a barrel of water. So the peasants came by the hundred, dragging their barrels of water up to the villa, and when the harvest came, the deal was honoured and the valley flowed with wine.'

Gigi, Imolo's first mate, was a silent man, and rarely joined in or commented on our endless conversations, but he interrupted to say:

'*El vino fa cantè e l'acqua fa piscè.*' ('Wine makes you sing, water makes you piss.') Then he was so pleased with his saying that he repeated it with a drawn-out '*Udiiio!*' of appreciation.

The workmen came to seem like a natural extension of our family. The absence of any doors beyond the kitchen wing bred familiarity. The foreman was Imolo, followed in the hierarchy by Gigi. Then there were two, three or four bricklayers and plasterers, depending on the job that day. There were also the electrician and the electrician's mate, usually to be found at ground level grappling with the immense and intricate lighting system that he had devised, for the house had begun to fulfil the workmen's fantasies. Questions like 'Would you like a one-way or a two-way video screen at the gate?' were already on the electrician's lips before there was any thought of a gate, let alone a main one. I tried in vain to explain that we were aiming, at this stage, for the bare necessities, but the workmen had other ideas. The Villa Orsola was the grandest villa in the neighbourhood and they had set their hearts on bringing out all its grandeur. There is still no gate, and there probably never will be, but somewhere under the caked mud, sunk a regulation metre deep, there are video cables standing by.

Having lost the original fireplace, which technically put the vendors into breach of contract, we were reimbursed a small part of the purchase price. It was this initial stake that had allowed us to start work on the villa. The first job had been to clean out a hundred years of rubble and rubbish and bird and bat droppings. The second task was to prepare two rooms, the existing kitchen, and build a bathroom on the ground floor for Allie and the Beauties.

So light and water were brought up the hill. A bathroom was carved out of a corridor, and sanitation made its début at the Villa Orsola. The child and I divided our days between applauding Imolo's efforts on behalf of our ruined house and contemplating its intricate network of roofs from a grass promontory to one side of it, discussing future plans and throwing imaginary parties.

The finished price of the first stage of work had fallen well below the original estimate, leaving a minimal sum of money still in the kitty.

We decided to make a tentative stab at the first floor. It was at some time around then that a process took over our lives and began to push us along on a wave of gathering force. The first thing to happen was that the workmen became unstoppable; they attacked the ruin of the first floor with the tenacity of a set of bull terriers, they got their teeth in and refused to let go. They outnumbered us and our pleas of insolvency were met with derision.

It was unthinkable to them that we might have spent

our all in buying the place – who would buy a house they couldn't afford to do up? This was not the Italian way, no one in the village would borrow to buy, they all saved fervently, the memory of hardship was too recent. No one lived beyond their means, they economized instinctively on anything where actual money had to change hands. Only millionaires or lunatics would have bought our house. They had met us and liked us and seen that we were not lunatics, therefore, *per forza*, we must be rich. When we found ourselves unable to pay for the work started on the first floor, the *geometra* and the workmen all insisted that we defer the payment and meanwhile that work progress, slowly.

At that point, I suppose we could, and should, have called a halt, but fear of being unable to pay a bill in a country where to overdraw one's current account at the bank is a criminal offence with immediate penalties, and where any kind of official borrowing can take years, if not a lifetime, made me predisposed to defer to them. Imolo wanted to work on and, panic-stricken, I let him. The bills were modest, the work was beautiful and, while he drudged at it, I climbed into my own treadmill with Robbie as we struggled to pay instalments on his bills. At some point, as at any gambling table, the stakes got higher and our winning turned to loss.

We observed the workmen with awe and wonder, watching the alchemy they wrought on our house while fearing the outcome. It became a spectator sport. Windfalls were all instantly signed over to them, royalties and advances and all kinds of sales sank into that bottomless pit. It was like the Poet Laureate's property-buying theory in reverse. I felt despair and elation mix with the truckloads of cement: despair at the mounting debts, and elation at seeing an unfinished house moving towards its completion after a hundred years of being a sleeping beauty. On the few occasions when despair took the upper hand and Imolo found me weeping in one of the doorless rooms, he assumed that my tears were those of a frustrated housewife unable to cope with the clouds of cement dust, and comforted me with assurances that he would quicken his pace.

'Don't worry, Lisa,' he'd try to reassure me, 'we'll get the house ready for you soon.' And in vain I'd protest, while by way of diversion he would lead me off on an extensive tour of his day's work, with detours to highlight what lay ahead.

By June, Imolo's team and their guided tours had become a regular feature of our life. From seven in the morning until four or five in the evening, Monday to Friday, they would be there. No job was too small not to require a few words of praise. Every minute of every weekday was monopolized by his eager artisans. As the builders' aspirations rose, so did the size of the workforce. There was an elusive plumber and his silent assistant, who would often be cursed for being absent at crucial moments. Once the telephone was connected, it would often ring for the mysterious plumber, as other building sites and private houses tried to track him down. Since our job was his biggest, it was assumed that we had him hidden somewhere in the bowels of our new drainage system. Another regular member of Imolo's team was Luciano, the housepainter with one huge bicep, who would stand in the middle of a room eight metres square with a roller attached to a three-metre pole and paint the entire surface, including the ceiling, while only budging a matter of ballet steps. Luciano had a repertoire of songs from Walt Disney films which he whistled and sang from seven o'clock in the morning with relentless jollity.

Then there was the number one blacksmith, a master craftsman who came originally from the village but had later moved further afield. He took on the four floors of balustrading for the marble staircase. The number two blacksmith, seventy-year-old Gelsomino, lived in the heart of the village with his extended family. His father had helped to build the unfinished extension on the villa before going off to fight in France in 1916. There was also a stonemason with a mutilated hand and a slow delivery service, who cut and carved marble like a maestro.

The chief carpenter was a vast, wheezing gentleman with an extremely delicate manner. This soft-spoken giant would lumber up the open cantilevers to whichever floor he was supplying windows for and check every measurement at least three times. He'd gasp up and down the stairs, struggling with his emphysema while regaling me with the latest on the sorry condition of his overloaded heart. His work was consistently brilliant, but his health had a fluctuating graph. I could tell when he was back in hospital by the presence at the villa of his two assistants, who moved, worked and talked in sync. One was unusually tall and thin, the other was short and dormouse-like.

At nine o'clock in the morning, and at some point in the afternoon, there was a small party somewhere in the house or grounds as anything between two and twenty workmen knocked off to consume litres of local wine and take a rest. Most of them went home for lunch (a three-course affair) since they lived locally. But the plumber and his mate could often be found sitting in a corner, perched on a pile of rubble and chewing an entire salami apiece with half a kilo of unsalted Umbrian bread. Umbria defied the salt tax many centuries ago, and as a sign of solidarity with the past, the *Papalini* (natives of this former Papal State) still eat all their food undersalted and bake their bread without salt.

Chapter 6

Sant' Orsola crouches on the edge of a road that once stopped a few miles beyond the village boundary, petering into an almost impassable mule track. Thus no one ever went to Sant' Orsola by accident or because they were passing through. It remained isolated from most of what was good and bad in the rest of Umbria, let alone the rest of Italy. It became close-knit and interbred. Unmolested by travellers, bandits or even taxmen, the Orsolani developed no fear or suspicion of strangers. During the Second World War, their open, easy ways were sorely tried, but few reprisals were enforced upon them, despite the Partisan enclave, and the bombs that fell fell mainly by accident, intended for larger, vaguely similar targets.

Towards the end of the war, the village sheltered two American airmen and an RAF officer for over a year. These airmen taught the local children to sing 'She'll be coming round the mountain when she comes', so that when the Allied armies arrived they could sing it and thus disclose their act of kindness under German occupation. To this day, I catch many a strain of 'Singing aye aye yippie yippie aye', and I've often been asked to translate the refrain, which has enormous significance to many a sixty-year-old. It is always a disappointment to them that there is not more poetry in the lyric.

The hills around Sant' Orsola were full of Partisans. Men from the village lived out with them; the local barman was their message runner. As work on the house moved forward, more and more stories unfolded and more and more false walls emerged and were knocked down. Some of them still had mouse-chewed cobs left behind them from the days of the hidden grain.

Everyone who came to work on the house had a theory about it and another scrap of narrative to add to the ill-fitting jigsaw of its history. Soon, the workmen's visitors outnumbered our own. People came from all around to see Imolo's reconstruction of the villa. Each newcomer announced himself in the same way, yodelling up from the forecourt, 'O, Imolo!'

Everyone seemed to be connected in some way to the villa, which they called *il palazzo*. Dozens of local people were reared in the big kitchen, and so many people either claim to have been born here, or to be related to someone who was, that visions of a massive rural maternity ward take shape. However, the director of the telephone company was definitely born here – many witnesses stepped forward to corroborate his claim – and in honour of this, he jumped us along the queue for a new telephone line.

The *palazzo* also seems to have been a labour-intensive farm since the last war. The shepherds who kept sheep on the first floor came visiting, as did the swineherds of the pigs that once roamed on the ground floor, or those who fed the quail on the second floor. Others, looking as though they wouldn't know one end of a farm animal from another, wandered around nostalgically. These, I was told, just used to make love in the open spaces of the vertiginous attic, with its fourteen window holes open to the air, on a granulated mattress of bat droppings.

Imolo and the workmen speak of the past here as though it were tangible. They prize it the way the best wild *funghi* are prized and stored away to be savoured at will. Their memories are hoarded, pored over and then bottled up again. They are communal memories, stored in the *cantinas* under all the houses and cottages with the barrels of wine, and it's usually the wine that brings them out. Imolo explains that the days of poverty have come to an end in this part of Umbria, but they are often remembered. Tobacco has changed their fortune. Until 1945, the local men had to emigrate or work a six-day week as day labourers, charcoal burners or woodcutters in the endless forests. His family, who scraped a living as agricultural workers under the few local landlords, were the lucky ones, able to live with their families, and the women and children helped bring in the crops.

The land around excelled in no single crop, producing only inferior versions of what neighbouring Tuscany grew. Then the tobacco began to catch on, and from 1953 onwards there was a boom which by 1980 had provided every family in Sant' Orsola with their own house, a piece of land, and at least one car. So the wolf is far from each door, but psychologically it is still there, hovering in the garden, somewhere between the lilies and the lettuces.

The older generation all have bowed backs and gnarled, scarred hands. Many of them wear the black and dark-blue garb of 1900. The old women wear headscarves and thick wrinkled wool stockings, regardless of the heat. They gather immense bundles of faggots to stoke their stoves and bread ovens. At dawn and dusk they can be seen hobbling along the edge of the road with these bundles on their backs, while their grandchildren whizz by in their new Fiats. These grandparents are all quite well-to-do, despite appearances, but their wealth has arrived too late to change their ways. They live in the same houses as their grown-up children, surrounded by luxuries and all the gadgetry of modern technology, but they cling to their old cycles of ritual behaviour, working long hours on their own allotments and vineyards.

Sant' Orsola is an organized village, run by a junta of local men and women who form the *proloco*. The *proloco* raises money from within the village and then spends it on dances and banquets, picnics, concerts and fireworks. The women gather mostly in each other's houses. The teenagers travel in packs of cars and mopeds, cruising from disco to disco, while the men congregate at the four local bars and play cards. They play a game called *briscola*, and another called 151, both governed by strict rules that include (Italian fashion) rules about permissible cheating. Four players sit around a table thumping their cards down dramatically, while a group of advisers and detractors stand by them, shouting advice and recrimination. On Sunday afternoons, the men dress up to play Italian bowls – *bocce* – with heavy balls which they roll down a long sandpit. No game is complete without its crowd of loudly arguing umpires.

The parish of Sant' Orsola sprawls across a long river valley and straggles up the wooded slopes of the hills to either side. There are dozens of hamlets, or *frazioni*, all belonging to the village. The centre of the village is enclosed in a triangle formed by the church, the bar and the *campo sportivo*. After a few glasses of the local San Giovese wine, anyone will tell you the secret that they share at Sant' Orsola: Umbria is the centre of the world, and Sant' Orsola itself is the good heart of Umbria. This is not strictly, geographically, true, but the point is not worth arguing. The vicinity of the Tuscan border is irrelevant, just as the vicinity of lovely cities and the approach of the twenty-first century are irrelevant. I thought when I lived in Venice that I had found the proudest people in the world, but here, without any of the Venetians' snobbery, are the proudest people. They make no concessions to other places (mostly unknown); this is the best, the first and finest. As an essay in positive thinking, it seems to have worked. The village has such a pleasant atmosphere that all over the neighbourhood, potential rivals will say quite spontaneously, 'Sant' Orsola *è bello*, eh, there's no place like it.'

Despite my years of brainwashing here, I have to say that it is not actually the most aesthetically pleasing village in Umbria. But its spirit is *bello* and I happily concur that there really is no place like it.

In the 1950s and '60s when work was still scarce, and all but the landowners were grindingly poor, dozens of men and boys emigrated to Switzerland to work. Thus it is sometimes called a Swiss village (of which there are many, hereabouts). Imolo told me:

'I went to Switzerland too. It was there that I learnt my precision. It's a cold place there, people are cold inside. I was lucky, I met a family who took me in. I think I would have died if I'd had to cope on my own. It was hard.

'After Switzerland, I moved to Milan. I used to work on old *palazzos* and churches.

'Most of the villagers who went away suffered out there. Our children will never *have* to leave, like we did.'

Imolo has two children, as do all the couples in Sant' Orsola. The families are planned (in strict defiance of the Pope). He told me one evening, down at Regina's bar, toying with his empty wine glass and a battered cigarette,

'In other villages, the children leave now not because they have to, but because they want to. That is what we're trying to balance here, I suppose.'

Chapter 7

On June 3rd, the two-roomed flat on the ground floor was plumbed, wired, drained and painted and the two Irish Beauties and Allie travelled down by train from Venice and took up residence there. Allie had managed to keep his secret about the ruinous state of our villa until the final taxi ride from Perugia Centrale station. Then his excitement got the better of him and he regaled the Beauties with the horrors they could expect. It was a good tactic. They arrived so apprehensive at the thought of making their beds in a concrete mixer and eating their food off the floor that they were charmed by the spartan flatlet. It was not how they had imagined the rather grandly termed 'staff flat' they had been offered months before when we were all in Venice, but it had furniture of sorts and it was newly whitewashed and there was glass in its small, deep-set windows.

Imolo, Regina, Gigi and the electrician had all turned out their gardens and *cantinas* to come up with some rudimentary furniture. The two rooms and the long kitchen had a cell-like quality, bare and high and cool.

Allie was delighted with his room and with the progress made on the general clearing of debris from the rest of the house. And Imolo was delighted with Allie. When work stopped for the day, he asked permission to take him down to the village.

'*Sembra un'angelo,*' he said over and over again, and for once this didn't embarrass my very shy son. In fact, Sant' Orsola cured his shyness. Imolo kept him under his wing, initiating him into the intricacies of wet cement and plumb-lines, teaching him the local dialect and how to be an ace *briscola* player. Imolo paraded him proudly from house to house, showing off his perfect Italian, his quickness at picking up the Castellano dialect with all its Orsolani variations, his cleverness with numbers, his golden curls and his sailor suits. It was Allie who charmed our way into the heart of the village. Only nice parents could have such a nice child. Our apparent lack of respectability was for-given and the little world of Sant' Orsola opened up to us in ways we had never hoped for.

The child Iseult had already found a place for herself on the back of many a moped. She had made friends with the son of the Sardinian shepherd further up our hill, and her nights were spent disco dancing with a gaggle of teenagers from the village, travelling in convoy across the Umbrian countryside from one glittering dance floor to the next. She shared this circuit and her new friends with the Irish Beauties, and the three of them spent their afternoons in extensive preparations for the coming night.

In a traditional neighbourhood of extended families and unbroken marriages, we landed as though from another planet. Here we were, a family of all women and children. The Beauties quickly went down in local lore as distant cousins, since the concept of au pairs was an alien one. The idea of paying babysitters struck our neighbours as comical; to do so on a camping site, however grandiose, struck them as absurd. To avoid further confusion and tangled explanations of how we had met (through the advertising pages of *The Lady* magazine), we settled for kinship.

The biggest confusion arose over the identities of the child Iseult and myself. We are alike enough to be mistaken for one another (in a dim light or through dim cataracts). This caused numerous misunderstandings. Why was Allie's mother out dancing until all hours? And why was she careering around the countryside with all those teenage boys?

Perhaps the worst of all our crimes against propriety was brought to light by routine officialdom. Italy is a land of bureaucracy. Nothing can be done, installed, connected or transferred without filling in forms in duplicate and triplicate, accompanied by passports and birth certificates. Names and surnames are listed and repeated endlessly. Since no one person in our household bore the same surname, our forms filtered back to Sant' Orsola on a wave of conjecture and scandal.

It was early June when Robbie returned from Scotland, having buried his father in the windy cemetery at Keith. His arrival made our household seem respectable. It didn't matter how many women there were, so long as they had a *capo casa*. Imolo was a man's man and he defected instantly to try to bond with Robbie, whose forays into the world of local or any dialect were blind alleys at that early stage. Imolo was deaf to all pleas of incomprehension. He sought out Robbie to share his wine and to explain the finer points of each day's labour.

Taking his lead, all the workers began to defer to Robbie, trying to shoehorn him out of his daytime solitude. Robbie navigated the front and back stairs to his advantage, making full use of the diverse exits and entrances to evade their frequent queries. Since he made all the main aesthetic decisions on the villa, he didn't see why he should have to be bothered by hourly queries and inanities. I found Robbie hiding in the long cupboard under the back stairs. I found him scuttling from one communicating room to the next on the first floor. I found him hiding on the upstairs loggia, and once, the plumber found him flattened against the roof. He had been pursued right up to the top of the villa and in desperation had escaped through the tower.

'Artists are strange people,' the plumber would announce thereafter to anyone who cared to listen. 'Robbie looks for inspiration face-down on the roof, risking his life for it.' I found him there one day and he told me himself that he was searching for *ispirazione*. I've been on a few roofs myself and I never guessed that inspiration lay under the tiles.

Gradually, I persuaded all but the plumber to leave him in peace. I explained that not only did Robbie not understand their technical language, but he had little interest in details, and much as it went against the grain, they would just have to make do with me. Imolo was never really convinced by this, believing that Robbie understood these things better than me, as one real man to another. The drawings of what had to be done were in Robbie's hand, and he wanted Robbie to pore over them with him. The plumber continued to pursue Robbie, trying not only to ply him with questions about his work but also about the nature of inspiration.

All the single and the lascivious members of the work-force tried to entice the Beauties into the hills after working hours, but with little success. Their social diaries were full. They had discovered the local football team and had been officially enrolled as mascots. Their time was almost entirely taken up in teaching the village team and its reserve bench how to drink whiskey by the half pint, and how to dance the latest Galway jives.

To this end, they set off each morning wearing lurid mini-skirts, a great deal of war paint and costume jewellery. Ostensibly, their mission was to buy bread for the family picnic. The Beauties were soon such a success in the village that they rarely returned in time for our lunch. The Orsolani had never come across such pale, grey-eyed women, certainly not ones who were taller than they were and could beat them at arm-wrestling. One of the Beauties spoke some Italian, the other had none. Undeterred, they communicated via the language of sexual tension and their sheer determination to have a good time. The Beauties were girls to be reckoned with, and Sant' Orsola reckoned agog.

After the initial flirtations had been dealt with, they were taken from house to house to meet parents and grandparents and to sample the wine from each householder's vineyard. Amazon in their bravery and exotic in their finery, they were initiated into the mysteries of all the local *cantinas* long before the rest of us. The Beauties were vague about these outings, from which they returned staggering, their ash-blonde heads numbed by liquor.

'They ask us a lot of questions about you and we just sort of fill them in as best we can.' This embroidery remained, a cobweb of guesswork and fantasy intended to smooth our way but actually digging hidden pitfalls for a long time to come.

The Beauties returned to our half-starved establishment with tales of plenty:

'Somewhere under every house there are oak barrels of wine. There are vats and pipes, and iron hooks with raw hams hanging in veils of peppery mildew. They carve the ham wafer thin, and the salamis, and they offer it to you with slivers of honeydew melon fresh from the fields.'

Often as not, the Beauties would return without any bread at all, lurching up the drive at around teatime. They jealously resisted any attempts to wrench the lunchtime shopping trip from their otherwise empty agenda of household chores.

'You should see the sides of streaky bacon and the jars of best steak sunk in oil and herbs. And do you know, they have hundreds, but hundreds, of bottles of tomato paste

53

stored up. We are to go to the next boiling session, in August, when the tomatoes are so plentiful nobody knows what to do with them if not bottle them up with garlic and basil and olive oil.

'We're getting a taste for the olive oil.'

Their staying power at the wine-tasting sessions in the dank *cantinas* became legendary; invitations arrived from all sides for the statuesque Beauties to inspect wine cellars and the strings of plaited onions and mushrooms and walnuts bottled and pickled and stacked on rough shelves. They spoke of pots of quince jam, and chestnut honey with its slightly bitter undertow. Each time they gorged themselves down in the village *cantinas*, they returned determined to diet and lose several pounds in time for the next night's disco. Thus bread and other carbohydrates were always the last thing on their minds as they set off with their shopping lists to forage for our daily rations.

Having trudged up and down the track in sweltering heat so many times already with the child Iseult, we were reluctant to set off after them to collect our bread. Each lunchtime became the triumph of hope over experience, resulting in meagre meals served on crackers eaten out in the rubble on our checked tablecloth.

Meanwhile, the Beauties knew the various merits of everyone's *cantina*, including Imolo's and the other workmen's. They sampled last year's wine and the vinegary dregs of the year before's, and the sweet strong *vin santo* made from raisins. Having first ostracized the workmen, they became quite friendly through a drinking acquaintance with their parents and grandparents, and chatted happily about *cantinas* in their pidgin Italian.

Whenever Imolo enquired as to the Beauties' whereabouts, we told him wearily that they were down at the *cantinas* and he tossed his head happily.

'Money is all very well, but it's only paper, and the

Church is for special occasions, but food and wine are the religion of every day.'

Noticing that we seemed to live off crackers, Imolo kept extolling the merits of the local bread. 'Get the girls to buy it,' he'd say, as though life were that simple. He advised, and we waited hungrily. Umbrian bread, like its Tuscan neighbour, has some astonishing qualities, not least its ability to turn impenetrably hard in a matter of a few hours. We discovered that it also made an excellent fuel brick, burning for an average of twenty minutes per kilo loaf without either smoke or smell.

Imolo, who never cooks, but can and will advise on all things culinary, knowing, instinctively, how to cook anything better than either his wife or me, told me that I should use our old bread to make *panzonella*, a local delicacy and once the staple diet of many an Orsolano. *Panzonella* is an acquired taste, with its chunks of raw onion floating in oil and soggy bread, but like bread and dripping, or beans and hash, it has a nostalgic quality that is untransferable.

By mid-June, we had reached a compromise: the girls went down to the village as though to buy bread, and we learnt how to make *ciaccia*, flat, leavened loaves cooked over embers. These fat pitta breads go very well with slices of raw ham and fresh pecorino cheese which we bought from the Sardinian shepherds further up the hill. The film of cement dust that had come to cover everything including ourselves enhanced neither flavour nor texture, but we got used to it. Our salads were brought in daily by the workmen and their wives. It was the season for the *insalata di campo*, a phenomenon that affects the whole of Italy. Entire villages crawling face-down in ditches are not, as they might at first seem, drunk, mad, or sniffing for magic mushrooms, they are scanning every blade of grass to detect the wild salads that grow with them. Young and old search through March, April, May and into June for the aromatic *marroncello*, the *grospignoli*, *radicchio*, *raponcioli* and *ginestrella*. Expert fingers claw out the *ragaggioli*, *lattughina* and *rucola*. Some of the above varieties can be found in the markets, but the Orsolani believe that the local varieties are best. There is a deep suspicion of all things bought, and a strong preference for barter. Food and tradition are inextricably locked together. For the Orsolani, the only good things that can come from outside their village are people.

Chapter 8

My childhood fantasy of musical bedrooms was coming true. Ever since reading *Orlando* one summer while a reluctant inmate of the children's ward at the South London Hospital for Women and Children, tied down by drips and tubes to a bed among many beds, I'd longed for a house where I could ramble from room to room, sleeping at random on unknown territory. Now our mattress and its accompanying sheet of polythene moved all around the villa in search of a resting place. During the summer, Robbie and I would move again and again, restricting our migrations to different parts of the house.

The main and most decorated façade of the house faced north and the north side of the villa was bounded by cypresses. This had been a disappointment to me at first, having grown up with the cult of worshipping south-facing windows, but as the temperature raced daily up towards 40° Centigrade, it turned out to be the best way of escaping the stifling heat. The south side of the villa looked over a vineyard and down towards the stone buildings of our neighbours. By mid-July we had tried most of the rooms, hot and cold, large and small, flirting with them and then moving on. Each time I found a promising skeleton room, I set up my board of trinkets, balanced on two blocks of terracotta purloined from Imolo's jealously guarded store.

With the trinkets on my board I put photographs and books. I made up our mattress with a Victorian bedcover and Venetian brocade cushions and I gathered a vase of wild flowers, dog roses or lingering broom to make myself feel at home there. The housemartins had arrived before us and wasted no time in choosing their rooms and making their nests. From dawn to dusk they swooped in and out of the uncovered window spaces, scattering their droppings over everything. At night as we lay in bed, their place would be taken by dozens of bats. I had to keep telling myself about the bats' infallible radar system, because they would dart so close to my face on the pillow that they seemed genuinely in danger of getting entangled in my hair. On the nights when there seemed to be bat conferences, and more than the usual swoops of bats would invade the room, I slept with a sheet drawn over my face.

Privacy being something from the past, it was often Imolo who awakened us in the early morning, getting in at six to have an early tour with me before his workforce arrived. He told me it was bad luck to sleep with one's face covered, but the danger from bats, mosquitoes and sometimes hornets forced me to ignore his warning. The hornets' domain was the north-west corner of the second floor and the entire third floor, where they remained until Imolo forced Gigi to burn them out.

This pre-dawn blitz was not 100 per cent successful. From our vantage-point underneath the offending room with a hornets' nest the size of a violin on its high ceiling, we could hear Imolo being the boss and chiding a reluctant Gigi to climb up a long stepladder with a burning torch.

'Get on with it, Gigi. *Dio buono*, they're only insects, they're not going to eat you, are they, they're not snakes you know, they're not tigers.'

'No, Imolo, they're hornets and they're going to sting me.'

'Don't tell me you're afraid of hornets!'

'I'm afraid of hornets, Imolo. Why don't you go up the ladder and I'll hold it?'

'No.'

'Why not?'

'No.'

'So you're afraid of hornets too!'

'Look, Gigi, just get up there, man, we've got a lot of work to get through today. I can't stand here all day waiting for you to get your courage up.'

'Why me, though, Imolo?'

'*Bé!*'

This was followed by a noisy descent, giggling, a return, a repeat of the dialogue and then a rerun of the entire process. On the third attempt, the dialogue was followed by a burst of blasphemy and some stifled whimpers. From the sound of footsteps running through the house, I deduced that the hornets were partially burnt, thoroughly disturbed and in hot pursuit of their attackers.

The elder of the Irish Beauties confidently told me that she was allergic to wasp stings and would probably die if bitten by a hornet. For weeks after the slaughter, the villa seethed with enraged insects. Twice a day, at dusk and just after dawn, I patrolled the rooms with a Chinese slipper, meting out destruction to the offending creatures, swatting them against the bare walls, two inches of poisoned stripes. Sometimes, a particularly brave or savage hornet would turn on me and divebomb me as I ran, forcing me to take refuge under a blanket for anything up to half an hour.

The house was full of intruders. Once we woke to find an electrician lying on our bedroom floor, marking out the rubble around our mattress with white paint. When I stared at him as though to say, surely this is an invasion of our privacy, surely we at least pretend and don't come through the open doors? he stared back at me with a winning smile, nodded '*Buon dì*' and got on with his measuring. To take an interest in a room was enough to make it interesting and the workforce gravitated and settled there like an inevitable cloud of dust. But the invisible barrier of the doorways usually held and the room would be occupied as we vacated it each morning.

Robbie and I awoke to the sound of a voluble assembly convened a few centimetres away from where our bedroom door would have been had there been one: immediate plans were being hatched to get the puffing carpenter up to make that particular door before any of the others, to measure the window, to order the shutters, to plaster the walls, lay a floor and to wire up every conceivable part of the room so as to be ready not only for the gadgetland of every thoroughly modern Italian home but also for the twenty-first century. By nightfall, our chosen room had filled by a process of dry osmosis with tools, sacks of plaster, buckets of marble dust and coils of plastic piping. We slept the uneasy sleep of trespassing vagrants.

At seven o'clock, sounds as loud and as various as those of a visiting fair came tramping towards us. Within seconds, they would be upon us, hovering by the gaping doorway of our surrogate bedroom, and Imolo, using the same decibels he would use to shout up from the ground floor to the tower, called, 'O, Lisa, come and see something.'

Imolo's idea of something could be anything. One day it was the discovery of another underground stash of the original terracotta needed to finish the façade. One day it was the unearthing of a scorpion's nest under a loose stone on the back stairway. Sometimes it was the detection of a flaw in our restoration plan, sometimes it was a mere hitch. And sometimes Imolo would get me up to admire the pools of pink sunlight that settled on pockets of hill-slope, highlighting the intensity of green that is so character-istic of Umbria. Imolo was in love with the crest of a hill behind the house towards a place called Zeno Poggio. I watched him watching it with rapture, and the lifting of the veil of constant sorrow that seemed to hang over his face.

As the summer moved on, Allie became a new Zeno Poggio for Imolo, which meant that from his arrival in Sant' Orsola, Allie led a charmed life. His days were spent 'helping' Imolo and Gigi, his evenings were spent down in the village playing games and cards, and his nights were spent in whatever bedroom happened to be within earshot of our own as we moved around the house. Where the child Iseult had spent her formative years on a sugar plantation in Venezuela, Allie had spent his on a train. He is the only one of my children to have followed me through an entire phase of the addiction to perpetual motion to which I occasionally succumb. So he is used to moving; and still regards beds somewhat as unnumbered couchettes.

Our original plan of having him live downstairs in the habitable flat with the Irish Beauties had foundered. We had not taken into account the almost constant absence of the Beauties themselves. With discos throbbing until three a.m. and the pizzerias mopping up the *après* disco trade until four or five, their hours were not the most suitable for babysitters. We had had, as a family, some singular failures among our earlier attempts to employ nannies, which had led us to the simple conclusion that two au pairs would be better than one. We had, in the past, lived (albeit briefly) with helpers so disturbed that no one could have lived with them. From this we deduced that if a girl already had a friend who was prepared to go abroad and live and work with her, neither could be entirely impossible or mad. Indeed, the Beauties were two extremely charming girls, and since their main duty was to stand in for me on the few occasions when I had to be absent, we were not unduly bothered by their relentless socializing while I was there.

Imolo, as Allie's jealous protector, quizzed me on the Beauties' obligations and chided me for failing to keep my house in order. I had become sufficiently friendly with the Beauties to trust them and to know that they didn't have whiskey-drinking competitions in my absence, and neither did they fail to rise before noon when I was away. Imolo did a lot of head-shaking over this particular domestic arrangement. The child Iseult once told him that the Beauties were angels compared to some of the species we had included in our human zoo in the past. Far from setting his mind at rest, this made him even more concerned about who and what would get to care for his little Allie.

Meanwhile, Imolo continued to call me out early each morning. He showed me a particularly rare wild orchid, the first of the field saffron, a finch's nest. When all else failed, he'd get me up to present me with a slice of cake and a plastic mug of home-made raisin wine. Whatever his reason, within minutes of the arrival of the workforce, I would be summoned, and part of the rest of each day from Monday to Friday was spent trailing behind Imolo and his gang of masons.

The child Iseult lived on the second floor in a relatively small room near the top of the main staircase. She chose this room upon arrival and didn't budge or agree to swap, and never lost her affection for it. In some ways it was the least habitable, having structural cracks in three of its four walls and very little by way of a ceiling. What few possessions anyone else had had a way of gravitating to-wards the child's room, borrowed and then lost under the accumulating debris of her clothes, things, magazines, and inevitable facepacks. On irregular cycles, the child trans-formed the unspeakable squalor of her room into a shrine of immaculate purity and order. It was clear that such days were upon her by her hair going up in a twist over her head, held in place by a toothbrush. Then, her clothes would be hitched up, her sleeves rolled and she'd get down to business. She took this business as seriously as she took her pleasures. On these days, her standards of hygiene and tidiness were so excessive as to make Italian housekeeping seem slatternly. This is almost a contradiction in terms, but such was the case. She would scrub, disinfect and polish every item in her room. In Venice, when afflicted by these zealous fits, she used to polish the bedsprings. Anything that looked even vaguely messy was thrown away. Alas, this usually included all those small missing objects so dear to my, Robbie's or Allie's heart. Books with dog ears were relegated to the black plastic rubbish sack, clothes that were torn or threadbare followed suit, anything, in fact, that was less than perfect or just aesthetically displeasing had to go, regardless of its worth, sentimental value or usefulness. Once the room was done, she could not bear to sully it, hesitating to crease her bed or tarnish her things with fingerprints.

When her energy had been thoroughly whipped up, it was liable to spill over from her room to other rooms, which she attacked with the same vengeful dedication. If the half-naked child appeared in the kitchen with a toothbrush stuck through her long curly hair, there was no peace for anyone. She scrubbed the floor on her hands and knees, laughing at her own fanaticism but in no way deterred. She became, temporarily, an eliminator of dust and disorder. If her energy flagged before her task was finished, a room could be left looking as though it had been hit by a cyclone. If her energy lasted, the room would have a sterilized, pristine designer look, and she was seriously offended if anyone tried to use it. These fits occurred, on average, about every three weeks. During the remaining time, her careless and slovenly behaviour reduced the rest of the family to despair. Trails of food, clothes and cosmetics followed her everywhere. Elements of the shanty town were never far away.

Imolo began to lecture the Beauties and the child Iseult on their shared tendencies towards squalor. He was genuinely puzzled by them, but found their eccentricities charming. He spoke of them fondly as of a rare breed of animal he had never come across before but now observed with curiosity. When he tried to interest them in the intricacies of his building work and it was to no avail, he didn't seem to mind. He had Allie's full and constant attention, so he was prepared to forgo the interest of the girls.

The one person he was really anxious to recruit was Robbie. Every evening, as Robbie changed into his finery to go down to Regina's bar, Imolo delivered a barrage of saved-up questions. This became so regular a habit that the final stages of Robbie's dressing became a court of petition. Imolo, clutching Allie's hand, would lean in the doorframe, I would be on hand to interpret, while Robbie fixed the studs into his detachable collar, tied his bow-tie, fastened his cuff links, donned a waistcoat from his extensive collection, then adjusted the fob watch and oval of lapis lazuli linked by a chain through the waistcoat. Imolo watched all of this entranced, gazing from the raw condition of whichever room we were in, with its ingrained cement dust and fissured walls, to the turn-of-the-century apparel.

It disturbed not only Imolo but the entire village that we had no car. It disturbed us. The relief, therefore, was general when Robbie's silver Panther finally followed us down to Umbria after an illness and convalescence in Siena. It was a source of continual entertainment to our neighbours to see how we could unfold not only our family but up to two friends as well from the apparently cramped two-seater sports car. Like pieces of a puzzle, we could lock ourselves into it. Once the car arrived, any lingering doubts as to whether Robbie was a power to be reckoned with were dispelled. Imolo declared him to be *forte*, praise which he had hitherto reserved exclusively for his favourite football team, AC Milan, and doubled his anxiety to have Robbie on his side.

After some complicated negotiations, juggling male solidarity against reality, a compromise was reached. Once a week, Robbie was press-ganged into a tour of inspection and, like a consultant physician being shown round the wards, the most delicate cases were saved for him and his will became law. When there was any serious disagreement, I held the ultimate weapon of translation, which I used with a certain ruthlessness, missing out bits here and adding a few flourishes there sometimes to guarantee the vote that suited me.

From the time of these weekly inspections, Imolo took to calling Robbie 'Maestro'. Being aware of the ludicrousness of his position, the Maestro played up to it, never making his rounds without first donning a fez for effect and grabbing a sword stick to point out his suggestions. It was only when he dressed in full Highland regalia one afternoon to make his tour that Imolo detected a hint of mockery under the madness. He cursed him roundly, and with as much feeling as when his beloved AC Milan lost a match. His revenge was to drop the tours of inspection. This should have been good news for the Maestro, but I think he missed his Byronic meanderings.

Chapter 9

By day, the Maestro painted in the wide open attic. Allie assisted with the building works, caking himself regularly in wet cement. Imolo began taking his clothes home to his wife Maria for laundering and then returning them in exquisitely folded packets the next day. The child Iseult slept until mid-afternoon, refuelling for the next night of gruelling pleasure. The Beauties also slept, comatose in their locked apartment with nothing but a radio playing to indicate there was life within.

Only Iseult could penetrate their slumbers. When she woke and wanted access to the one and only bathroom in the house, she would hammer on their doors and windows with such force that eventually the Beauties would stir. Before they deigned to unlock their den, the Beauties would scuffle with and shout at one another to decide who would get first use of the bathroom. They had learnt that once the door was open, Iseult would move in like an army of occupation. From the moment she set foot in the small shower room, not only would it degenerate to a state of utter squalor, but she wouldn't emerge again for hours. She was deaf to both pleas and insults. Grudgingly she might allow someone to squeeze past her and share the room, but no one could oust her. Allie had taken to bathing at Imolo's house, the Maestro and I had the use of the shower room at night, all night if we so desired, while the other contenders took to the dance floors of central Italy.

By day, I was being initiated into the world of stone. Floors, walls, sills, lintels, steps and stairs were all made of stone. There were stones everywhere, hindering the progress of the digger. I became a regular groupie at the local marble yard, assessing the various qualities, shades and shipping routes of each block of marble: shouting my requirements over the shrieking cutting machines in the workshop.

Whenever I played truant from Imolo and the overseeing of his work, it was to the wasteland of my prospective garden. I nurtured morning glory seeds in pots, and scratched in the rock-hard mud to make way for nasturtiums, larkspur and asters. I bought geraniums from the local florist and my first herbs: rosemary, thyme, sage and marjoram. I bought endless wet newspaper twists of sweet basil plants. I bought a pickaxe with which to penetrate the compacted gravel and caked clay that passed for a topsoil outside the house, and I planted and watered, coaxed and petted, a number of extremely sickly and unhappy plants.

Allie kept telling me that the corridor on each floor of the villa, joining the old and the new parts of the house, was sixty feet long. It was his great delight to play with numbers, to add and multiply and divide. He had measured every room, gap and crevice in the villa, he knew how many doors were missing and how many shutters, how many hundreds of metres of copper and plastic piping were needed to plumb, and how many hundreds of metres of cable were needed to wire. He spent his days counting. On the ground floor the corridor was open at either end and extended for a further sixty feet of pillared loggia, turning at a right-angle for a final forty-foot run towards the south and the vineyard.

This loggia was designed to run along two floors. The ground-floor loggia, when we arrived, was a not very cunningly concealed mantrap to the cellar, or perhaps a foray into scrapyard sculpture. Despite its primitively patched floor, the rest of the structure was in almost perfect condition. On the first floor, skirting what had been designed as a ballroom but was used as a grain store, the idea of a loggia was there, its finer points still missing. At the end of all the long, long lists of things to do, after all the etceteras, came the ballroom. We made exhaustive plans for it, and Robbie picked out the colours of the marble that might someday inlay its floor. He designed the exact shape and size of its boxed ceiling; triple-arched french windows appeared in dozens of the Maestro's sketches and drawings. I had walked across and around it endlessly with Imolo and the electrician, the carpenter and the marble mason. Its eventual completion was a task that everyone discussed but no one believed in.

I was more anxious to make a start on this lovely, derelict room than I was to have video screens wired up all over the non-existent garden. I lobbied frequently for work to start, albeit token work, on this the star chamber of the villa. Imolo was oblivious to my pleas; he continued on his own set course, altering it only for circumstance, the tardiness of the marble man's deliveries, and Allie. He dreamt one night that Allie fell through the loggia floor to the rocky cellar. The next day, he moved the cement mixer to the back of the house and began to churn up his mix, reinforcing concrete over the loggia floor.

The day after, much to Imolo's amusement, the Maestro and I removed the new lumps of concrete that had fallen at the base of the eleven pillars and took our pickaxe to the stone chips in what I envisaged as a flowerbed around them. We planted alternating jasmines and wisteria in the rubble at the base of each eighteen-foot pillar, so that one day the plaited stems would entwine and gnarl up past the intricate capitals of carved terracotta. They would grow gracefully over the balconies of the first-floor loggia that would lead out from the ballroom or drawing-room when Imolo had built them and it. They would fill the room with a heady scent. I explained all this to Imolo and the digger man (who had to be roped in to break up some of the worst rocks in our planting holes). I walked them through the dusty ruins, jumping over the craters dug by the mechanical digger and then left for future cesspits and drains, and other holes begun and then abandoned which were the failed excavations for the pipes of an aqueduct laid out at some point during the 1950s.

In the early evenings, a hush descended over old Sant' Orsola as the digger was switched off, the pneumatic drill ceased its quest into whatever piece of stone it was belea-guering, and the tile-cutter stopped whirring its blade through squares of terracotta. The workmen ceased yodel-ling, 'O, Imolo, show your face!' and Imolo stopped appearing at one of the seventy-two windows like a puppet in a country show to call down to his audience. A proces-sion of noisy Fiat 500s took off in the direction of the village, and we too left the house.

By six, the worst of the day's heat was over and the dirt road, called aptly in Italian a 'white' road, became navigable again with some degree of pleasure. Allie, armed with a life jacket, flippers and goggles, often set off ahead with the child Iseult to tackle Giovanni's lake, which had dried to the size of a pond. I would take the opportunity, away from mocking eyes, to tend my straggling herbs and flowers, fortified by the cloying scent of lilies which flowered valiantly through the strangling weeds. Then I followed my children down past the blue-robed Madonna in her shrine to meet them after their swim. They emerged blue-lipped and trembling from the lakelet which they shared with thousands of croaking frogs.

Following the track down to the small river that cut across the tobacco fields on our side of the valley, we were on the home stretch to Regina's bar. We paused to gather the giant sweet peas growing in clusters along the way and to collect stray porcupine quills. The last part of the road was lined by walnut trees. Over the main road, which was itself scarcely more than a tarmacked track, and up the facing slope was the bar. Regina's concession to summer trade was to place two long, rickety benches against the stone wall of her establishment and a white plastic table in front of them.

By half-past six, these places were all taken by a row of exhausted tobacco planters dressed almost entirely in rags. They slumped with their heads hanging down towards the hen-scrabbled dust at their feet. Drinking was strictly by rapid ingestion. No sooner was a drink ordered than it was swallowed in one gulp, and the empty glass handed back to Regina or the hovering Carlo, as though to remove all evidence that it had happened. Thus the tobacco workers appeared to be teetotal while actually getting very drunk. Two newcomers ordered up a tray of viscous white wine which they downed as though it were medicine and then the slump continued.

Imolo, Gigi and several of our workmen preferred to sit on a low stone wall to one side of the bar, marked out from the planters by their overalls and the cement dust in their hair and on their faces. They too were tanking up surreptitiously, and they too looked stunned by fatigue. At the arrival of Allie, Imolo shook off some of his fifty years and made way for him on the wall. A chorus of grunted '*Buona sera*'s' greeted our arrival. Regina laid aside the rabbit she was in the process of disembowelling and gave her hands a token rinse under the tap before serving us with blood- and bile-stained fingers. I knocked back a small tumbler of rough Vecchia Romagna brandy to relieve my own exhaustion from the hamster wheel that had fallen to my lot. Most of my life seemed to be taken up in a futile running in circles: an occupation almost as tiring as a hard day's work, but alas less productive.

As though by some prearranged choreography, the men all rose and jostled their way into the cramped bar, making as much noise as possible. Like a flock of starlings finding a wire to settle on, they organized themselves into groups of four players. The leftovers became unauthorized umpires as a session of serious card playing began. Imolo always got a seat, and he played with Allie at his elbow.

Up at the *palazzo*, we had a telephone line and a telephone number, but no telephone. We had been assured that the apparatus itself would arrive any day, with the emphasis on all the varying possibilities of 'any'. So I continued to make my business and social calls from the payphone in Regina's bar. This payphone was on the wall over a pile of sweepings from the barroom floor. Mingled with the dust, lolly papers and cigarette ends below were feathers and chicken's feet.

The child Iseult took advantage of the rush hour at the bar to place herself in splendid isolation on one of the newly vacated benches. The boys and younger men would gradually funnel back out into the evening sun to talk to her. By half-past seven she was joined by the Beauties – painted, adorned and ready for anything. Shortly afterwards, the Maestro Robbie arrived in a cloud of dust in his over-revving car, which he parked precariously on the steep hill. Several of the men jumped up to tickle his ribs and squeeze his elbows. He was offered free drinks but never allowed to buy any himself. (He drinks beer and they chided him for not drinking wine.)

From the high windows of the villa I could see over the belt of trees to the tobacco fields. I rose earlier and earlier, not only to be on my feet before the workmen's intrusions, but also to tend to my lilies and the two miraculous stems of morning glory that had fought off whatever epidemic had wiped out their peers. One of these morning glories had billeted itself on a dying plum tree in the centre of what would one day be my herb garden but was still a resistance hideout for a handful of tomatoes fighting on through the summer long after the last of the green beans and lettuces had surrendered unconditionally to the invading weeds. The purply blue of each morning flower twining round the crumbling black bark of the host plum tree filled me with pleasure. I have been fixated on morning glories ever since I can remember. My health and happiness are interwoven with the life-cycle of this South American climbing weed. I took it as a fine omen that two of my seeds had passed their survival test, and a personal favour that every morning I could step out and see a blue haze of delicate trumpets in my wilderness.

I looked out on the tobacco planters assembling by the river no sooner than the skylarks had lifted from the fields in speckled clusters. The field workers wore their uniform of rags, a unanimous and voluntary return to the weeds of the past as a way into the daily drudgery of the crop. I watched them divide into groups formed by families. The only two disqualifying factors for working the tobacco fields were death or total paralysis. Anything less disabling could not prevent the octogenarians from donning their tatters and bending over the tyrannical floppy-leaved tobacco plant. Old women bent almost double by scoriosis of the spine, with hands gnarled by arthritis and eyes bleared by cataracts, took their place in the file of lines bowing and scraping to the lord of prosperity. The long hours under the burning sun, the constant bending and the need to concentrate – for this labour-intensive crop, skilled selection makes or breaks an eventual harvest – prostrated the workers with exhaustion. But in the early mornings, they arrived full of energy and bright with jokes and banter. Their voices rose up the hill towards me as noise only, the meaning trapped in the clipped and slanted dialect of the village, a foreign tongue filtered through cypresses and birdsong.

Chapter 10

Sometimes as many as ten vehicles hovered outside the villa at night with their engines on and their stereos blaring. There was competition as to whose car would get to transport the child Iseult for the evening. Any time after dinner and after dark, there was a loud purring and a flashing of lights and beeping of horns from the machinery-strewn forecourt. Behind the cars, outriders on mopeds tried their luck. The young Orsolani travelled in a pack. On Friday and Saturday nights they stayed out until just before dawn, on other nights they returned earlier. Whomever the child chose to travel with, the other cars always accompanied her back home.

Having no electricity still in the main part of the *palazzo*, we relied entirely on candles. The child Iseult (like me) is afraid of the dark and insisted on being accompanied up the dangerous staircase by a bevy of young men. The local girls were too afraid of the place even to get out of their cars. The child kept a candle handy in the first alcove on the marble stairway, and by its flickering light she made her way up the wide hanging steps to bed. These stairs still had no balustrade, and cantilevered into nothing. The child's bedroom was forty-eight steps up and four turnings away. The greatest challenge, though, came in locating the three missing steps where a failure to jump and the subsequent drop would have resulted in almost certain death. Beyond the top stair, there was a stretch of corridor several metres wide where the lack of a roof had caused the structure to collapse. Only the most careful edging along a reasonably stable girder could get one across.

With a certain ruthlessness, once at the doorway of her makeshift bedroom, the child Iseult would barricade herself in and keep her candle. Her escorts would then have to rely on their own candles or torches. Torches never lasted at the *palazzo*. Like socks and pants in the weekly wash, they slipped into the fourth dimension and once bought were never seen again.

One night, having indulged in the local habit of sitting in their idling cars listening to music and whispering about life, art and metaphysics for several hours, the convoy of chaperons grew sleepy and turned tail and went home, leaving the child with a large-handed Adonis with a lisp. Adonis knew the *palazzo* well, he had visited many times by day and was confident that the perilous mantraps held no threat for him. At three o'clock he escorted the child to her room, where she fell forthwith into a comatose sleep. Armed with a candle and a cigarette lighter in reserve, Adonis set off downstairs.

It was a starless night and the stairwell was plunged into darkness, and so was he when his candle blew out from a stray gust coming through the roof. Relighting it with his lighter, Adonis was unnerved by a night bird swooping at him from the broken rafters. He dropped the candle and heard it hit base so far down as to frighten him. His lighter had fallen somewhere nearby in the rubble. On hands and knees on the landing, he set off in search of it, lost his direction and found himself hanging from the iron girder into the void below. Being a fit and muscular Adonis, he heaved himself back on to the ledge of what he recognized to be the long corridor. He remained calm; he knew the geography of the house, he could navigate a way out, feeling along the raw plaster and the stonework to the various doorways, counting his way to the back stairs.

Unknown to him, Imolo had been busy the day before, dismantling the upstairs props of indoor farming. Doorways that had been bricked up had been opened and one doorway that had been open for the whole of Adonis's life had just been bricked up. The more he edged along the walls, counting spaces, the more confused he became, until he lost all sense of direction and found himself walking into things. Finally, after he had clambered back on to the girder with his feet dangling into space again, he gave up and crawled (wrecking his Armani trousers) to a place of relative safety where he waited, huddled against a pile of tools, for dawn to save him. He stayed there for over two hours, whimpering occasionally as he nursed his cuts and bruises and his wounded pride. Several times I think I heard him calling, but the house was full of whimpering cats and whining stray dogs and night birds, so I kept turning over and going back to sleep.

I tried to persuade the child Iseult to get her friends to switch off their engines when they called for her, and also to call for her rather than persist in the particularly irritating habit of hooting their horns. Since it took her an inordinately long time to add the finishing touches to her extensive toilette in readiness for these outings, the purring and the beeping could go on for anything up to half an hour outside. My children, however, are very Italian, and both love the sound of throbbing engines and tooting horns. So the stillness of the night continued to be interrupted and the song of the nightingale perched somewhere high in a cypress tree was intermittently drowned by invading cars. More and more cars came in search of the child Iseult, and also of the Beauties. Long after they had gone, little fleets of hopefuls still turned into our rocky drive.

Ever since the end of May, the property had begun to resemble a rustic car park. Anyone looking for *funghi* in the woods around us knew the *palazzo* and was used to parking their car there and maybe changing into their wild-mushroom-hunting costume in what was supposed to be our garden. At weekends, there would invariably be cars in front of the house by the time any of us awoke. I tried to catch the parking offenders by rising at dawn, but it seemed that they arrived even earlier. I tried asking the child if the cars were there when she got back from her discos, but she was too dazed to know. I asked the Beauties, but they were too tired to know. So the car dump grew. Imolo began to mutter about putting up a gate, but since there was no fence or wall and the land fell away in places on bare rock, revealing several different points of access where bulldozers had munched their way through the hill, it was hard to know where to site anything quite as formal as a gate. Allie decided to charge people for coming on to our ground. He spent a weekend drawing up a sign with ten thousand lire painted on it in burgundy enamel. He then spent many hours multiplying cars by ten thousand to see how much money he could make per week, per month and then per year. He fell out with his sister when she refused to charge her admirers an admittance fee. On the Monday morning, Imolo erected Allie's toll board at the edge of our bumpy track under a struggling olive tree.

Having put up the notice, Imolo discovered that some of his tools were missing from the derelict store room on the ground floor. All the workmen then went through their tools, which revealed a number of petty thefts. Imolo took the law into his own hands and revved off to the village in his chipped, canary-yellow Fiat 500 to find number-two blacksmith Gelsomino. Twenty minutes later they returned, Imolo still looking affronted and the aged Gelsomino looking decidedly tipsy. Imolo stomped and consulted and then ordered a movable iron bar of the kind used at frontiers and level crossings.

Because of the stream of visitors to the workmen, to the Beauties, to Iseult and to us, the frequent deliveries of sand, cement, stone and tools and the more frequent errands to the village and back by one or other of the workmen, this arrangement soon proved impractical. There was a great deal of creative cursing in which the name of the Madonna was linked to all the usual farmyard animals, with some more exotic additions like 'Madonna boa constrictor!' Then Imolo compromised, shrugging his beige-overalled shoulders and shaking his head as though to imply that to lift the barrier ·would be to lift the gateway to hell; an act that he personally could not be held responsible for. While the padlocks were removed by the obliging Gigi, Imolo excavated another crumpled cigarette from his top pocket and sat on a large stone to smoke it. After that, the bar came down only at night and at weekends. This served to keep the sightseers and the mushroom pickers at bay, as well as any potential thieves or bandits. A side effect, which I feigned to regret, was that the nightly invasion of escort cars could no longer idle their engines in the garden-to-be.

Undaunted, the long nights out continued. Number-two blacksmith Gelsomino was a weatherbeaten seventy-year-old with a mischievous smile and a frequent pout like that of a young boy wanting to be kissed. His son, Leonardo, was scarcely out of his teens and looked as though he had just stepped out of a fresco by Piero della Francesca. He had his father's lips, and the Beauties and the child spent many evenings with him and his friends on the disco floor.

'Don't you get tired, dancing all night?' I asked him one day when he came up to assist Imolo in his bricklaying.

'But we don't dance all night,' he pouted. 'We go to different discothèques in different places. It's a long way to Rimini, you know.'

'Ah,' I said, not really the wiser. Rimini is on the coast. But the regularity and the lateness of the outings had aroused my curiosity. They seemed dense with flirtation but devoid of any overt sex. Also, Sant' Orsola seemed to be a village where most of the inhabitants equated leaving the parish boundaries with stepping off the edge of the earth. The only exceptions were the disco dancers, aged between fifteen and twenty-five, a gang of single and indefatigable dancers. Not only that, but I knew the child Iseult rarely had any money and the Beauties 'worked' for almost a pittance, so what they had could not have stretched to the high cost of tickets and meals. Drinks were probably no great expense for the child, at least, since she formed part of the Coca-Cola brigade. Like many of her local contemporaries, her idea of a stiff drink was half a litre of fizzy orange.

'Who pays for all your meals?' I asked her one afternoon as she rose from her slumber, 'and how do any of them have enough money to treat you to dinner every night?'

'They don't treat me to meals, Mamma,' she said. 'They pay for my entrance to the discos and that's all.'

'Well, what do you eat then? You always make a point of missing supper before going out.'

'I get car-sick, Mamma,' she told me. 'We cruise all night in convoy. Sometimes we go to Rimini and sometimes we go to Perugia. We go to Florence and Siena, Arezzo and Foligno. We go into a discothèque for about ten minutes, then we get into a huddle and everyone argues about where to go next, and finally we set off for the other side of Italy and it takes three or four hours to get back. They all drive so fast, and the roads are winding. I'd be sick if I ate anything.'

'And do the others enjoy cruising? They must do, I suppose.'

'Oh yes, they all love it. It's just that I get car-sick.'

'Then why do you go?'

'Because I'm young and I want to be part of the village, and actually I sleep most of the time and just wake up by the sea or in the centre of Florence. I like it.'

Allie had been many times to dinner at Imolo's house. He knew his wife Maria well and was on *briscola* terms with both of his children. The Beauties were also well acquainted with Imolo's house, although they seemed to know his *cantina* and its contents better than the upstairs. But it was a big day for Robbie and me when Imolo formally invited us all to lunch. This was our first introduction to the world of Sant' Orsola beyond the confines of our hamlet and the bars and shops. Imolo's homestead was on the outskirts of the village, on the hem of another hamlet set into the rocks and rockroses.

Maria d'Imolo (as we called her to distinguish her from all the other Marias) was plump and fair and so anxious to please that her words tumbled out breathlessly. She looked much younger than Imolo, with whom she seemed to have a close but bantering friendship. Her shoulders were strangely lopsided and she scuttled around her kitchen like a broody hen as she served not a lunch but a banquet. First came *crostini*, thin rounds of toast spread with piquant sauces, followed by Maria's homemade *tagliatelle*, produced with the help of her daughter, who was the child Iseult's age. The third course was chicken roasted on a spit, which was followed by rabbit and then roast pigeon. For dessert there was a rich, sweet, *mascarpone* cream with coffee and Marsala folded in, and lastly pears with pecorino cheese.

Imolo found fault with every course but the pears and cheese, over which he waxed lyrical.

'Eh, sì,' Maria chided him, 'the pears are only lovely because you grew them.' Then she turned to me and confided that Imolo was never satisfied at the table.

'He would cook everything better if you listened to him, but the trouble is he never cooks anything, he just complains.'

Imolo grinned, unrepentant. 'Eh, la Maria is living off her nerves today, she's missing *Beautiful*.'

I discovered later that *Beautiful* was a soap opera, running into many hundreds of episodes, to which whole sections of the village were addicted. They gossiped about its characters as though they were all Orsolani and some of the women had heated arguments over their impossibly tangled affairs.

After our coffee, which was served in Bavarian gold-leafed cups brought out ceremoniously from a glass-fronted cabinet in the unused dining-room, Imolo gave us a grand tour of the *cantina*. His basement wine cellar was stocked against the forked ills of inflation and disaster. Imolo and Maria had four rooms used as larders and a lemon house, which in winter was almost entirely taken up by a single lemon tree, one of the seven wonders of the neighbourhood. The climate is too cold in Sant' Orsola for oranges and lemons to grow outside, as they do on the Italian Riviera and further south. So lemon trees are grown in terracotta pots and then taken into protective custody for the winter.

A *limonaia* at a grand Florentine villa is often an equally grand conservatory, but a lemon house here is usually a dark room with a wide doorway to get the giant pots through. It is often windowless, like Imolo's. The pots, varying in dimensions, are frequently so big that it would take four men to lift them. They are kept on individual trolleys. Imolo's pot was an old iron cement mixer; and that, he said, was why his lemon tree was better than others: it drank the iron. When he took us down to see it, it was in full flower. He seemed as pleased with it as a proud father. His usually rather serious face beamed as he broke off a sprig of heavily scented blossom for the child Iseult, and then another for me. I feared it might damage his production of lemons.

'Eh, *no*, eh,' he assured us happily, 'nothing can damage my lemon tree, it gives nearly a hundred lemons. Think of that. A hundred lemons.' He thought a little and then said, 'You should have a lemon tree, Lisa.' Then he thought a bit more. 'But it wouldn't be like mine. What do you know about lemon trees?'

We were still outside his house as he denigrated me at some length on the subject of citrus farming and failure. Once inside, his manner changed and he became a host of infinite tact and kindness. Despite his much-vaunted yodelling, which was audible from valley to valley, Imolo had a deep, quiet voice when he consented to talk one-to-one. His eyes seemed to hold an infinite sadness and depth, and his nose had been broken many times. It was not particularly swollen or scarred, it just looked as though it had decided not to bother to stand out from his face any more, so as to lessen future bashings. Instead it folded down from the bridge. The effect was not unprepossessing; it looked like an exaggerated version of a Roman statue.

Imolo and Maria spoke so fondly of Allie, I felt as though they were trying to persuade me to let them adopt him. Allie himself was obviously used to hearing such praise from them – he was at home in their house and with their children and things. He exchanged cryptic messages with their son in the local dialect, drawing yet more praise. There were no other children in our hamlet, all the rest of them lived in the village proper. Although he had managed to lose his shyness with the adults, by doing the rounds of Imolo's cronies and playing endless games of cards with the village elders, Allie was still loath to venture among his peers. He would be going

81

to school with them in September, and he had decided to wait until then before making friends of his own age. He was still missing his best friend from Venice, a boy called Gabriele del Corso, to whom Allie scrawled postcards which he never sent.

Imolo would not hear of his beloved Allie squeezing into our two-seater Panther on a full stomach with the rest of us, and insisted on driving him home after lunch. So Allie and I and Imolo set off in his best car, leaving his workday Fiat 500 tucked into the brambles at the side of the road. During the short trip back, Imolo harangued me about the sorry state of my vegetable patch. To neglect this *orto* is almost as serious a crime as to neglect one's children.

When we bought the villa, a lady asked if she might keep on the small allotment behind it for the first year of our stay. She told us it had been hers for years. We had readily agreed, as we would later do to so many things, hoping to find favour with our neighbours. For most of that first year we were either abroad or in Venice, so it was really only since our arrival in April that our interests had clashed. The lady in question climbed silently over her fence of bedsprings, old gates and sheets of beaten tin to tend a minuscule patch of garlic. She invited us to help ourselves to any that we wanted, but I had never dared to put her generosity to the test. Embarrassment had clearly made her reluctant to use the barricaded allotment properly, and when she officially handed over the plot in late May, it was too late for us to plant the patch and she had missed out on growing all her summer vegetables and salads, too. Only the morning glories, whose seeds I had bought in an ironmonger's in Scotland and then planted surreptitiously, had thrived. The seed packet said that they liked waste ground. The two plants that survived gave an instant thumbs-up to mine, tangling up through the mounds of goose grass to blossom on the diseased plum tree. Imolo found their profusion offensive in a vegetable plot and advised me to pull them up and squander no more time and water on them.

'You'll have to do a proper job in the autumn. You should have thought about it earlier. It's a disgrace.'

My mitigating plea that the ground had been on loan was dismissed as a feeble excuse.

'It was ridiculous to agree to such a request. Now where is your own *orto* for the summer, and where is hers? Not, of course, that you are not welcome to any of my salads. You've seen how much we've got, but you should have thought about it for yourself.'

I found it particularly galling to be told the rudiments of good husbandry and gardening, when the latter had long been not only my hobby but my great delight. It had been my dream for so many years to have a proper garden again that I felt eaten up with impatience. My hands were still metaphorically smarting for having failed such an elementary test as a lettuce patch, so I did not elaborate on my horticultural fantasies. Instead I thanked him for his and Maria's hospitality and led Allie over to contemplate the lily buds with me.

Imolo's parting shot, reverberating across the valley, was to remind us to attend something to which we had now been invited so many times that the entire family was bubbling with expectation:

'Don't forget to come to the *festa* of the Madonnina del campo . . . all of you, the girls, the whole household! You won't forget?'

'We haven't forgotten.'

'Sunday lunch.'

'Yes.'

As the car turned the first bend, he came back into earshot.

'*E allora*? Will you all be there?'

Chapter 11

The *festa* was to fall on the third Sunday in June. Imolo had
been talking about it for weeks. Every day when he came
to work, he called me aside and mentioned this *festa* as
though he had just discovered it on his way uphill to the
house. In the week between our lunch at his house and the
festa, my right elbow was bruised by the frequency of his
confidences on the subject. Meanwhile, the only signs of
any preparations were verbal. But two days before the
festival of the Madonna of the fields, the usual choir of birds
calling from the trees, shepherds calling from the surrounding fields and woods and workmen calling to each other
across the *palazzo* was joined by a strange series of cackles.
On closer inspection, I discovered the source as the yard
behind my neighbour, the Signora Maria del Gallo's house.
Half the noise was coming from a gaggle of geese and
ducks and a disconsolate huddle of chickens who were
waiting to be slaughtered in a makeshift pen. The rest came
from a circle of old women who were sitting on upturned
oil cans around a bonfire, upon which a great iron cauldron
had been set to boil. One of the women, whom I had seen
earlier working in the tobacco fields and who seemed to be
related to Gigi, was telling a story in response to which one
of her companions was braying like a donkey, locked in
such laughter that she was in danger of falling into the fire.

The distinctive smell of wet feathers and singed quills wafted up across the vineyard for the entire morning. Allie, whose sensitive soul still had to be blindfolded to walk past a butcher's window, and who would not eat if he inadvertently saw meat in the kitchen, was so disturbed by the squealing and squawking that we tried to convince him the birds were being vaccinated rather than strangled. He believed us because he wanted to. When he was safely out of earshot, ferrying coconut oil up to the sunbathing Beauties, Imolo told me:

'Killing, plucking and gutting fowl is considered woman's work.' I had noticed that any man who gave a hand and showed any skill was praised for it and even a little admired, as though he had given birth or performed some other unnatural feat. A few of the men in the village were described as being 'just like a woman', a reference to their ability to pluck and gut chickens.

Preparations for the festival had begun in earnest. After work, the men erected a scaffold and canopy at the wayside shrine. The tall, gallows-like construction was hung with a bell. Two lorries laden with planks and trestles, linen and crates of fizzy orange churned up the dust and then parked beside the old Nicasi barn on the second bend in the dirt track that led to our house. The excitement was contagious. Allie began to behave like the child Iseult, turning out his suitcases as he changed from one sailor shirt to the next and struggling into every pair of shorts and trousers that he owned. He was Italian enough in his ways to know by the tender age of six that a *festa* meant dressing up. Imolo had said there would be other children at the *festa*, which had thrown him into a fit of panic vanity.

The child Iseult, fired with enthusiasm for the coming festivities, took the unprecedented step of dismissing her swains and staying in for an entire night. We ate outside under the stars, in a flattened space between high stacks of floor tiles. The moon was nearly full and, with its pink aureole and the host of fireflies, the light was softer than that given by our usual candles. When the batteries ran out in our ghetto-blaster and cut off the Puccini arias we had been listening to, we carried out the wind-up gramophone that the Beauties had kindly lugged down from Venice, and took it in turns to crank up its gravelly two-minute tangos. We made some abortive gestures towards playing charades, but the night was too languorous and just too dark to see the nuances of anyone's performance. So we sat and talked until two in the morning and then took to our various mattresses.

When I rose at seven, I found that Allie and the child Iseult had both risen before me. Allie was busy gelling back his hair, sleeking his ringlets into the lounge lizard look. The child was bubbling over with energy. She was wearing nothing but a pair of cut-off jeans and a toothbrush through her hair. She had moved every movable object out of the kitchen and the floor was awash with cloudy suds.

'Sorry about this,' she said, wading through the stirred cement water. 'I got up with a *labastida.*'

A *labastida* is a Latin American Spanish word meaning an inexplicable and usually pointless action. It comes from the de Labastida family, a clan of Spanish noblemen who intermarried through pride and ended up so inbred that their actions were of an inanity bordering on madness. The child Iseult was descended on her father's side from a long line of de Labastidas.

We ate our breakfast of peaches, cream crackers and honey with hot milky coffee on the island made by the stone hearth of the raised fireplace. By half-past eight, the child had finished scrubbing and rinsing. By nine, the stone floor had dried back to its original cement-dusty patina. By nine-thirty, the Beauties had emerged from their beauty sleep and were dressed up and raring to go. We waited impatiently, joined after ten by Robbie in a white linen suit with a gold brocade waistcoat. For some reason, all of us had chosen to wear white, as though anticipating a first communion.

At eleven o'clock the bell clanged on its gibbet, carrying its summons to us on its way round the valley. We set off down the dirt road strewn with yellow petals. Buckets of broom flowers gathered from the surrounding hills had been scattered all the way down to the shrine. The sweetly scented petals were thickest around Maria del Gallo's house and on the bend past the ruined Templar tower outside the Cenci household. And they were thick by the barn where the communal lunch was to be served. A crowd was gathering, coming across the field tracks from all directions to gather at the shrine.

Don Annibale, the shrunken priest, was already there, accompanied by a Franciscan friar in his brown robes and sandals, and an acolyte with a surplice over a lime-green tracksuit. A small kitchen table had been placed in front of the statuette in her shrine. On it were a battered and faded painting of the Madonna, a vase of wild flowers and a crucifix garlanded with daisies and speedwells, which Don Annibale proceeded to hold up.

Old men in Sunday suits that seemed impossibly stiff made their way to the shrine, walking slowly under col-oured umbrellas. Some of the suits seemed to walk by themselves, the wearer having shrunk inside them. Of all the local men, age had whittled the most flesh from our neighbour Cenci's bones. He had long passed the stage of thinness and entered the realm of the skeletal. His skin was disturbingly transparent, his head unnaturally long. In many faces among the crowd gathering by the shrine, a pattern of past malnutrition could be traced.

Some of the nicknames reflected this. As the locals

87

greeted each other, I discovered that the animal terms the girls had given to people they'd seen but whose names they didn't know were, in fact, their names. They squeezed each other's shoulders and held hands or kissed, and said,

'Oh, Snake Head, how are you?'

'I'm here, Fish Face, so I can't complain.'

'Oh, Rabbit, where have you been?'

'*Dio buono*, Turkey. And you?'

The bestiary unfolded with cockerels, lizards, dormice, lice and the like; names all fondly given.

Cenci's extraordinary features defied any analogy with the animal kingdom. He was unique. His skin hung in a series of folds, as regular and as consistent as an attempt to recreate the famous Fortuny pleats on human skin. Not only was his head long, his face had a narrowness which scarcely allowed his features to fit into it. His translucent, pendulous ears reached down past his wrinkles almost to the stiff collar of his shirt. From under the wide serge cuffs of his capacious jacket, two massive crimson hands emerged, attached to the bird-like bone of the wrist by what looked like the flimsiest connection. The fingers were mangled by arthritis, twisted into knots and stumps. The veins stood out and throbbed in a necessary testament to his continued animation. It was hard to believe that anyone so apparently frail could live.

Cenci seemed unaware of his death-defying appearance. He smiled beatifically at anyone who would catch his eye. The Beauties told me that he was always ready for a glass of black wine. He still made his own, together with his lifelong friend Gianni, and his own wife, Nunzia. They had barrels and barrels of it in their *cantina* and would waylay people on summer evenings to come in and sample it. The child and I had stopped on our rambles a few times to greet him, but he'd seemed flustered and shy. Now he said,

'Why don't you come and see us again? Your boy comes to us with Imolo a lot . . . Will you come?'

We all assured him that we would.

He whispered to Robbie, 'Come for the wine.'

Allie translated for him from the thick dialect.

'Simple but good!' Cenci called out in his high trembling voice. He shuddered and sighed, '*Uddìo!* It's so good!'

This was followed by a slight scuffle as his friend Gianni rummaged for his microphone, got it up to the artificial voice-box in his throat, plugged it in and then grated out in a Dalek-type voice, 'Eh, *sì*, eh!' which was his favourite expression. Having said it, he put the process into reverse, unscrewed the microphone, covered up his throat grid with a square of gauze which hung conveniently, a grubby curtain around his neck, and replaced his microphone in his pocket until such time as the need to concur audibly gripped him again.

Cenci's movements were slow and awkward as he made his way up to the Madonnina. There was a faint pink glow on the otherwise colourless furrows of his face. There was to be a party: a gathering in good faith. He was excited. His pale, watery eyes darted across the crowd, lighting up at each face he recognized. He was among fellows. They had laboured together for seventy years. As children they had scoured the hillsides and rivers for nourishment and fun. His memories and theirs were shared.

He came back a step towards us.

'I was the gardener for forty years at the other villa in Sant' Orsola. The one owned by the doctor who sold you the *palazzo*. Eh, *sì*, eh, but I've grown too spindly for that, and the doctor has let the garden go, which is a shame. I entertain myself looking after my vines now, and planting potatoes, and the rows of maize on the edge of the vineyard beside the *palazzo* are mine,' he said proudly.

Imolo had told me that, unlike most of his peers, Cenci had bought neither property nor land. His ambitions were all turned towards longevity. He was greedy for life, despite all the weevils that had taken up residence in his three score years and ten.

The child Iseult told me that she had visited Cenci before. Unlike me, she wasn't shy, and didn't wait for invitations. She said, 'When he gets in from his vineyard, he climbs into an inglenook and sort of balances his bones on a bench. The kitchen is black with smoke and so is the fireplace, and he and Gianni sit and stare and chuckle at each other. There's a pot of water hanging on a chain near the back of the fire, and a smaller tin can which Cenci spits into under his seat. Once I found myself staring at him. You can see through his head. He could see I was wondering how he stayed alive and he said, "*Sò na cèrqua*" (I'm as strong as an oak). He's such a sweetheart, you should go and see him.'

As the procession moved towards the bridge and the river, I watched Cenci progress, a happy man living on borrowed time. Regina had told me that arthritis, pneumonia, pleurisy, emphysema and cancer had all lurked under the folds of his desiccated flesh. As he made his way laboriously down to the river, swinging his leg bones out from his locked hips, he continued to smile at all and sundry. He whispered to himself, chewing imaginary tobacco in his mouth made empty by the loss of his teeth. He kept muttering through the service. I imagined him saying: '*Sò na cèrqua, sò na cèrqua.*'

Cenci's wife, Nunzia, bustled along beside him. Despite his slowness, she managed to give the impression of finding it hard to keep up with him. She was in her seventies, but she looked far younger and had the airs and graces of a young coquette. She tilted her raddled head from side to side, clutching a traditional navy-blue cardigan to her fallen chest with one hand and holding a small yellow umbrella covered with orange poppies in the air with the other. She was between Cenci and Gianni. Cenci was mouthing, Gianni was battling with his microphone and voice-box, while Nunzia prattled on, half to herself and half to the moving crowd. Nunzia and Maria del Gallo were the grand duchesses of this *festa*. It was held on their road, the meal was served in the barn at the end of Nunzia's garden. Maria del Gallo never came to the *festa*, though; she told me she had not put in an appearance since her brother-in-law had been struck down by a stroke twenty years before. So Nunzia was the queen of the proceedings. It was her day, her chance to catch up with all the scattered families from the hills and take them into her smoky kitchen after the lunch, while Cenci and Gianni held court in their shared *cantina*.

There was excitement in the air. The skylarks had risen to it, the nesting finches paused to investigate. Above us, Maria del Gallo was on her balcony, wearing her Sunday best (navy-blue), framed by cascades of geraniums. Despite the tolling of the bell and Don Annibale's intoned prayers, there was a lot of taking of the name of the Madonna in vain coming from the men who were roasting the pork and the chickens up above. Their voices carried and the assembly at the bend of the road laughed at the profanity. Nunzia made a face and shrugged, giggling. It is a local pastime, this blasphemy or *bestemmia*: the application of a bestiary to religious icons. It is viewed with indulgence and some pride by the congregation of *Papalini* (descendants of subjects of the former Papal State). The Vatican ruled its states harshly and kept its peasants down, using them ill until 1861 when the Unification of Italy was more or less complete. There is still an affection for the Church, and religion is deeply rooted, but so is the instinct to prune its power; not to be overawed into servility.

We were made to feel welcome as we tried to merge with the crowd. Allie had become the pet of many households. Nunzia and the Signora Maria both kept a little stock of sweets and fizzy orange to persuade him to stay. He took little persuading. As the crowd of all ages formed itself into a loose procession, Nunzia was delighted to show her friends how close she was to this new child.

'We're old friends,' she announced to no one in particular, and yet loudly enough to carry over both Don Annibale and the distant blasphemers. 'He comes to my house most days, don't you, Alessandro?'

Allie was too shy to reply. Not wanting to contradict an ally, he stayed close to Nunzia as a mark of his allegiance. But no matter what she or anyone else asked him after that, he kept silent, caught in a paroxysm of embarrassment.

Eventually, Nunzia turned her attention to Robbie and me. We moved towards the river with the slow crocodile, voyeurs at their ritual. Don Annibale intoned while the congregation followed him towards the bridge, whispering its responses, '*Gesù perdonate le nostre colpe!*' Nunzia, seeming to sense our unease as infidels in that most intimate of ceremonies, kept up a running commentary intercut with her prayers.

'It's our Madonnina of work,' she whispered, 'she protects the fields and the fruit of our work. *Gesù perdonate le nostre colpe.* We ask for forgiveness and she looks after our corn . . . And the potatoes. If it wasn't for the Madonnina we would have terrible potatoes. They go all slimy. The old Madonnina was stolen during the war. We used to have to walk to the empty shrine every year until this one was put in, in '54. It was a homage . . . *Gesù perdonate le nostre colpe!* . . . These are the prayers of us Christians.'

At the bridge, Don Annibale stopped. His acolyte, a small boy whom I had seen many times doing wheelies on his bicycle on the road under Regina's bar, rubbed the dust off his new Reebok trainers against the back of his calves and swung the incense. The elderly Franciscan friar alternately bowed his head and raised it to the cloudless blue sky, moving his lips silently and consistently out of synchronization with either Don Annibale or the congregation, as though offering his own prayers. It had the effect of a scene from a foreign-language film, dubbed, as they all are in Italy.

Don Annibale lifted his emaciated arm to the four points of the compass, holding up his cross to each, warding off evil. He then spoke of plagues, as though he knew the horrors of each named torment. He looked easily old enough to have known everything personally, whether it was lightning, storm, hunger, sickness or war, flagellation or earthquakes.

'Deliver us, Lord,' he called out, crucifix outstretched, and the tension was such that I imagined a bolt of lightning striking him down-then and there on the narrow bridge. It was one of those miracles by default: Don Annibale was not struck down, there was general amazement and relief as he lived to turn the procession of gaudy umbrellas and lead it back, after a little tactical confusion as the tail of the winding serpent became its head, to the shrine and the waiting canopy.

In the intense heat of the midday sun, I felt as relieved as Nunzia and all her friends. At the moment of invocation, even the small boy in a large red baseball cap who had been running in and out of everybody's legs impersonating a hornet had paused. And a gaggle of girls in very tight shorts and halter tops, who had yanked the child Iseult into their midst and then shuffled along giving their responses and eyeing up the local talent and discussing their sexual preferences, had thrown down their chewed gum and remained as motionless as a group of upturned faces in a fresco.

Back at the shrine, Don Annibale said mass and gave a short sermon about dwindling rivers and dwindling congregations.

'Just twenty years ago, there would have been hundreds of people at this mass. In each of the cottages scattered across the hills,' he said, waving his diminutive right arm in a sweeping gesture that almost sent the wild flowers flying, 'as many as thirty people lived. Those cottages are empty now. This valley has survived so many trials in the past, but trouble was more recognizable in those days, it didn't wear a mask.'

Communion was served, and during the relative silence that accompanied it, a wail of '*Dio buono!*' echoed down the hill from one of the cooks. A whispered discussion took place as to the culprit. Several of the cooks and servers were immediately exonerated, on the grounds that the expletive was much too mild for them.

'Eh, *Dio buono!* That one would have brought in at least a pig or a dog.'

'Or a porcupine,' Cenci piped in.

'Eh, *sì*, eh!' A general consensus of agreement arose and drowned out the last few words of Don Annibale's blessing. Then the crowd turned towards the barn and the drifting aromas of lunch.

Chapter 12

The Orsolani have raised the preparing of popular banquets to an artform. They have studied, over hundreds of jugs of their heavy Trebbiano wine, every aspect of their preparation and presentation. They organized themselves into teams of those most fitted for each angle of their overall plan. One man prepared the three-metre long grills on their stands, burnt the sticks down to charcoal and kept the supply of extra fuel. Another marinated the lamb, chicken, pork, duck and pigeons to be grilled. Another (irreplaceable) figure was Giacomo, the meat chef. His skill was such that he was in the greatest demand. He took to his role with all the grace his massive frame could muster. He was six and a half feet tall, and his shoulders were so wide that, when seen from a distance, they gave the impression of a huddle of men stooping over the grilling meat. He was the only man in the village who could beat the more muscular of the giant Irish Beauties at arm wrestling. A vacant grin never left his face.

Three other men, Imolo among them, were in charge of bringing down animals for slaughter and then dismembering them. Imolo was one of the few people in the village of either sex who was squeamish about killing animals. He quartered and disembowelled them but balked at taking their lives. Anything feathered was deemed, of course, to be woman's work and had to be despatched by the female hit squad. Maria del Gallo, Nunzia and a friend were the meat-sauce makers for the first of the pasta dishes. It was their pride and skill. Maria d'Imolo specialized in the chicken-liver and giblet paste boiled with celery, onions, garlic and parsley which was spread across the ubiquitous *crostini* – ubiquitous, because every meal in Umbria contained somewhere in its first two courses of *antipasto* three types of *crostini*. These thin rounds of bread were spread with tomato, red peppers and garlic, or *funghi* (laced or not, as the season dictated, with truffle), or the liver *fegatello* as above. The word *festa* – whether it was a party, dinner, meal, first communion, christening, wedding, picnic, cocktail, or in fact any kind of entertainment whatsoever – instantly conjured up three types of *crostini* followed by two kinds of pasta and meat.

Our initiation into the local menu had begun with Maria and Imolo, where it had followed the rigid pattern laid down by hundreds of years of tradition. The landless *contadini* would have savoured such meals three times a year. Firstly, at this lunch, given in the olden days by the *padrone* to his field workers on the day of the Madonnina of the fields; then on the saint's day of the patron saint of the village; and lastly, at New Year, when every household, however poor, celebrated their Christmas with a feast. And a feast begins with three types of *crostini* . . .

Every time I sallied into the more public world of the village, I discovered some further aspects of our private life. At that first banquet I discovered that the child Iseult had fallen in love, not as one might imagine with a local swain, but with the local version of *penne al pomodoro* (short pasta tubes with a fresh tomato sauce). I had to restrain her physically from falling on the serving dishes being carried around by two be-aproned housewives. A passion that had begun with proffered lunches in the village blossomed and developed to such a degree that, to this day, the dish is still her staple diet. Perhaps memories of that initiation into the possibilities of sheer volume account for the vast quantities of the stuff she later cooked up at the *palazzo* when left to her own devices: *penne al pomodoro* sufficient for an entire army, or an entire gathering of Orsolani.

The barn had honeycomb-hollowed terracotta bricks in lieu of windows. These pierced it with cool pink light on three sides. The brick floor was strewn with broom flowers that mixed their scent with the strong wine that stood in vats by the door. Imolo tried to make Robbie feel comfortable by telling him in a stage whisper that the wine had been donated by the family who were once lords of the manor and owners of our house. He pointed out several of the gentlemen of that once illustrious but now dwindling family seated around the trestle tables. Robbie understood not a word of this and tried to get the Beauties to translate for him. Only one of them spoke Italian and it was not the one he chose. It took up the first three courses of the lunch to settle the ensuing confusion to everybody's satisfaction.

Large unlabelled bottles of wine were handed up and down the tables passing barricades of fizzy water and fizzy orange on their way. I sat across the table from Beppe del Gallo, and sandwiched between Allie and Robbie. Imolo kidnapped Allie almost before the meal started, and Robbie was busy unravelling the riddle of the wine, the barn and the *palazzo* with anyone who cared to clarify the problem.

Beppe del Gallo kept a half-apologetic smile on his thick lips. He had the expression of a naughty boy caught scrumping by a favourite uncle. His skin had the purplish hue of a potato eater, compacted in Beppe's case by his gleeful fondness for his own purplish wine. After fifty years of agricultural drudgery (mostly in the grasp of the sharecropping *mezzadria*), he had retired. As with most of the other pensioners in the neighbourhood, this had in no way daunted his efforts or his energy. Age merely slowed him. He could still be seen from dawn until dusk tending his rented vines outside our back windows, or his own patch of vegetables. He told me,

'We've borrowed a long strip of field this year and ploughed it up. We'll have *grènturco* (corn) to market, too. At the end of the year, I'll have sacks of potatoes . . . a lot of them . . . to sell. I've got watermelons along the ditches.'

When the drought came, and the tobacco workers were sweltering in the fields, he would have a stock of watermelons to sell them. The thought of all this future wealth and cunning pleased him no end. He had cheated his destiny: he was not going to die a poor landless peasant. He leant across the table and put his broken-veined face nearer to mine.

'Last month a porcupine got into my broad beans. Did he come up to you afterwards? Did he go for your beans?'

I wished that I had had some broad beans to have been gone for by anything as exotic as a marauding porcupine. With the general air of *bonhomie*, it didn't seem like the moment to divulge the sorry state of my garden. Instead, I assured him that no porcupines had crossed the vineyard on to our land.

'Eh, *no*, eh!' he said, looking around him to bring in his neighbours: Gianni with his microphone to his right, and a member of the snake-head clan to his left. 'Eh, *no*, eh! But do you know what a porcupine is?'

His companions were on cue and all three men began to describe different characteristics of the beast. Had I not known what a porcupine was before, I would have come away with a strange impression of an animal bigger than a dog but smaller than a horse, with a series of crossbows under its skin capable of launching quills of up to a metre long across distances so great that no one could agree on their length. I was momentarily left out of the conversation as the men discussed several important porcupine credentials, then Beppe del Gallo turned sheepishly to me and said,

'One thing I know about porcupines is that I caught one one night down by the bridge. It must have weighed eighteen kilos. We roasted it. It was really good. I can't tell you how much we ate that night! So much! *Uddìo.*'

We talked and drank and nodded until the surrounding birdsong stopped and a chorus of crickets took its turn. Three brothers from over the hill beyond our house had linked arms to steady themselves and their inner burden of wine. The middle one, an old man with a stringy face and eyes like raisins, tipped back his head and sang dirge-like love songs in a tremulous wail. He stopped half-way through and stared at his large clumpy boots.

'Go on,' the handful of people remaining encouraged him.

'Go on,' I said too.

Allie cleared his throat and looked embarrassed, making it clear that he for one felt no urge for the singer to continue.

'Go on,' the other brothers urged.

The singer shook his head slowly. 'I used to have a great voice, I used to sing at the harvest. But I lost it,' he said, and stared fixedly at his feet as though he might just possibly find it again if he looked hard enough.

The child Iseult and the Beauties had left with a throng of other youths some time before. They reappeared at the barn door looking hot and sweaty.

'Come on,' they said.

Their arrival worked like a signal for the more sober of our company to stagger out. Allie took this opportunity to pull Robbie and me to our feet, and we too left and made our way back up the hill. As we tottered past the vines with their blue sheen where copper sulphate had been recently sprayed, and past the lines of sprouting maize and the dusty brambles, the strangled cries of the renewed love song followed us, caught in the still heat.

After the festival of the Madonnina, I began to feel more able to wander in and out of people's houses. I took to visiting my neighbours with Allie as my password. Robbie and I strayed further into the heartland of the village, past the confines of Regina's bar to a second bar, a calmer and less bizarre establishment draped with Virginia creeper.

Some of the farmhouses *en route* were so rambling that I could imagine getting lost in them by day, let alone by night. It was the custom to build on a large scale. I was much more used to the higgledy-piggledy crofts of Liguria, perched on the edges of cliffs or on whatever precipitous ground was available just out of sight of the sea and the Barbary pirates. Then I grew familiar with the huts and cottages of many other parts of rural Italy. In Venice, families had lived like perfectly packed eels in incredibly confined spaces. There had always been grand villas, of course: the villas of Tuscany and the Veneto, but with few exceptions, these were not where we had spent our time. One of the surprises of Umbria was the sense of space, inside and out. Seemingly endless expanses of forest rolled into the skyline, and massive stone houses on three or four floors housed as many families, often more, each comfortably accommodated in high, big-windowed rooms.

Thanks to our days of walking up and down the road, we became very aware of the state of the crops in the fields and such things as the condition of the ditches. Having set aside my writing during the early months of our stay, more through necessity than choice (there was too much confusion), I took refuge in the memory of my previous career as a farmer. It was fifteen years since I had left the sugar plantation and avocado farm that I had married into the Venezuelan Andes; but our moving to the country-side seemed to have brought my closeness to the land out of hibernation. I watched the avenue of walnut trees and the gradual progress of their green and speckled fruit with a professional eye. I noticed the leaf curl of Nunzia's peach tree and the leaf burn on the newly transplanted capsicum peppers, and most of all I noticed the growing yearning in me to sow and reap.

The weather had lodged itself firmly in a heat wave. The Beauties were looking marginally less attractive as their sunburn peeled and blistered. The child, who like me has a naturally dark skin, was burnt to a deep cinnamon shade that she compared daily to Allie's less diligent tan, and Robbie's almost as spectacular hue. Spending most of my days indoors with Imolo and the workmen, I became, for the first time, the palest member of the family. We still ate our lunch in the garden-to-be and persisted with our tepid al fresco drinks, while beginning to recognize the absolute necessity of shade. Our minds turned to pergolas and bowers, covered ways and wide-leaved trees.

My initial plan for the garden, sketched out at least a hundred times with all the appropriate lists of plants, had to be modified to take in this new factor. The two gardens that I had restored in Norfolk had had their ancient trees, and reconstructing them had been more of an archaeological dig than a creative act. I had never made a beautiful garden out of a building site. Even in Venezuela, where I had started virtually from scratch, it had been the scratch of an internal garden bounded by colonnades on three sides and an immense avocado tree on the other. My ideas for Umbria were a mixture of the English country-house garden and a tropical fantasy.

I realized that it was too hot to want to walk along an English-style herbaceous border (if I ever managed to make one) unless there was the guarantee of a shady seat and probably a fountain at the end of it. I am, by nature, an unathletic person, so these considerations became particularly important to me. In my imagination, after the debris and the hard work of laying paths and beds and the planting of trees, cuttings and seeds, I saw myself lolling back in an Amazonian hammock with a cool drink and a shady spot to read. It was sometimes hard to transform what the bulldozer left in its wake into the idyllic place that would replace it even in my own mind, let alone anyone else's. I worked at it, though, forcing myself to believe in my dream. When I talked about it, which was rather often, my family humoured me. Robbie even helped me to make new plans for the garden, incorporating shade and structural shelters from the sun.

I took to making mental notes, month by month, of what grew well and what was merely surviving in other people's gardens. These were limited. The typical Sant' Orsola garden was made up of trees, grass, a handful of flowers, a huge vegetable plot and perhaps a vineyard. The two Marias grew more flowers than most. Flowers, like fowl, were cared for by women, and their destination was the cemetery.

I watched my morning glories bloom and fade and the clumps of lilies soldiering on towards their flowering time. I watched the swarms of butterflies that congregated over the more numerous clumps of stinging nettles, and I dreamt of the armfuls of flowers that would one day replace the rubble. Meanwhile, I compromised, planting palm trees, roses, hibiscus and oleanders in terracotta pots.

A flock of bedraggled Sardinian sheep rang their neck bells in a strange, picturesque symphony one day as they made their way down to a hayfield above the river. The next day, I called the family to come and admire their seething river of ivory wool gliding down the hill. The day after that, we all went out to the bar with the Virginia creeper to play table football and didn't return until after dark. By the next day, the contents of my six Sienese terracotta pots had been shorn to bare earth. I took the defeat very personally. As the sheep returned that evening, shepherded by a savage-looking Sardinian and three equally savage Sardinian Maremmano dogs, I harangued them all in a fit of voluble rage. The dogs completely ignored me. The shepherd listened for a few seconds and then did the same, wandering off with his limping sheep while I shouted after him. I pushed through the sheep to pursue him. He looked both bored and utterly unrepentant.

'I'll kill them if they come in again, do you hear?'

Imolo had followed me out and pulled me back.

'Lisa,' he warned me, 'don't mess with him, he could be dangerous. Come on,' he said, guiding me back by the shoulder into our slope of broom. 'He doesn't understand Italian, only Sardo dialect, but the sheep are a cross we all have to bear. Come on.'

Chapter 13

I was in the kitchen marinating chicken breasts for our nightly outdoor grill, turning the pale slices over and over in olive oil, thyme and white wine, when Imolo came in, so excited that he had to sit down on one of the oil drums we used for chairs.

'We're connected,' he said, clutching one of my oily hands in his. In all the weeks of our enforced intimacy, he had never made a pass at me and I somehow felt he never would, so I waited for him to calm down.

'Lisa, we're connected! Come with me, come and see.' He led me out of the kitchen and along the long corridor newly patched and reinforced, with its swathes of grey plaster waiting to be painted and scars where electricity, gas and water pipes and cables had traversed it. He took me to the square bathroom he had been working on for some days with the plumber and his mate.

'Now close your eyes.'

When I opened them, there was electric light in the room and water running from the taps into the washbasin.

The cupboardlike affair of the downstairs shower room in the Beauties' flat had become increasingly difficult to use. Life seemed too short to queue behind the child Iseult and the Beauties themselves who monopolized the cubicle, and the squalor of the flat had increased in direct proportion to the time they had lived there. Ever since Allie had come upstairs to live with us, the flat had become the abode of dirty laundry, the six unhousetrained kittens, their little dishes of forgotten and decomposing food, and all the accoutrements of a beauty parlour. The arrival of hot and cold water on the first floor, together with sanitary arrangements of the kind one tends to take for granted, brought an entirely new standard of living to the Villa Sant' Orsola. It was such a luxury to have a proper bathroom, with the added comfort of a lovely view filtered by cypresses, that we began to get a foretaste of what life might be like if we ever got any furniture and doors.

A large red-velvet curtain from our Venetian flat was nailed over the bathroom doorway. We covered an oil-drum with a lace cloth to put our toiletries on. There was a shower which gushed over the newly tiled floor inlaid with Carrara marble. One day, there would be a Victorian bathtub beneath this shower. But that day seemed to get no nearer. I was getting nowhere, rather laboriously, with the Port Authorities in Livorno. We had three forty-foot containers impounded there, containing not only the cast-iron bathtub, but forty second-hand doors and all our furniture and furnishings. Every day, I called Livorno from Regina's bar and complained, insisted on and begged for the release of these things. Since the ship had docked and they were unloaded seven weeks before, nothing had happened that could be interpreted as even remotely positive. It seemed pointless to let bureaucracy ruin our first summer in Umbria, so we introduced certain creative touches in the improvised furniture line, filled our rooms with wild flowers, and enjoyed our house despite the lack of usual trappings.

Once the tobacco crop was safely planted and had been coaxed from limp seedlings into upright plants, and the corn was growing, and the hay was safely baled, there was a lull in the valley which was pleasantly reflected in the relative quiet of every evening. Straying an extra half-mile to the second bar, we met a number of new Orsolani. The second bar was always known as the bar, as though there were no other, either in the village or in the hazy area beyond its limits.

The bar was tended by Menchina, a doll-like lady of an indeterminate age. Menchina suffered from migraines, and had done for the past forty years. On days when these headaches were at their worst, she wore a red bandanna tied around her forehead. After forty years of service in this bar, she treated it as an extension of her own sitting-room. The bar was often empty for many hours at a time. When the adjoining shop was shut, and there was nothing else to do, Menchina played patience at one of the three indoor tables. She played sometimes for hours on end. Her voice was husky and very sensual, her movements were nervous and quick, although each thing she did was completed slowly, hindered by her excess of nerves. Partly through long bouts of loneliness in between bouts of much company, she often talked to herself or to her daughter's mongrel lap dog, Giada. Giada was one-quarter chihuahua and three-quarters attention seeker; she was intensely jealous of Menchina's affection. Menchina reasoned with her as though she were a full-sized recalcitrant adolescent.

As soon as I met Menchina, we made a friendship of flowers. The edges of the terrace outside the bar were the fruits of her labours: a potted garden after my own heart. I recognized at once the efforts of a thwarted horticulturalist. Each skirting rose and shrub was crowded in its space by pots of rare lilies and strains of camellias, gardenias and begonias. On the narrow stone steps at one end of the terrace that led to her dwelling above, hibiscus, azaleas, hydrangeas and agapanthus lilies competed for the meagre light that managed to pierce the canopying vine.

Life under this vine was peaceful, and in a most addictive way. We began to spend as much time there as Menchina spent at her patience. Next to the terrace was the bar, and next to the bar was the village shop. There, if time was allowed to follow lazily the pattern dictated by both climate and tradition, fresh bread, pecorino cheese, drinks, fruit from Menchina's orchard and wine from her husband's cellar could be bought. It was also the general sorting office for gossip, which Menchina culled and redistributed, pressing her fingers together in an attitude of prayer, straining the chipped crimson varnish of her fingernails in her efforts to be fair.

Whenever a baby chanced to be brought into the bar or shop, Menchina held up a painted thumb and persuaded the child to take it, then she whirled him or her around the composite marble tiles, always humming a snatch of the same polka, always dancing the same steps and seeming to remember some long-distant time before there was ever a need for a red bandanna, or the patience of endless solitary games.

At night, at the villa, after the workmen had left, leaving a trail of tools and half-finished work, and after our trip to the bar and to the telephone at Regina's bar to call the Port Authorities about our furniture, a calm settled over our space. It was a calm so beguiling that it even managed to ensnare the child Iseult and the Beauties from time to time. At those times, the calm might be punctured by their effervescence and yet it prevailed, and they too were charmed by the scent of the three flowers on the lemon tree in one of the plundered terracotta pots and the clambering jasmine I had lured into another. Frogs and crickets croaked and sang from every direction, and more stars than I had ever seen lit up the Umbrian sky.

We had grown used to sitting out in the evening, fleeing the penumbra of the house. When the electricity arrived, delightful as it was to be able to plug in our record player and use an electric refrigerator and immersion heaters, and illuminate the stairs, the light in the big kitchen seemed disturbingly bright at night. We missed the fireflies and the proximity of the nightingale as it kept its vigil. Screech owls were nesting in the coppice of young oaks in our grounds, some forty yards from the villa. Their milky droppings splashed over the high grass and their alarm shrieks echoed through the night. The absence of furniture was less discomforting when we sat outside: if anything, the forecourt was overfurnished, filled as it was by Imolo's crates and piles of materials and the two sentinel cement mixers.

Locally, the moon was a subject of constant discussion. Many of the farming activities were governed by it, as they had been in Venezuela. When the planters sat around in Regina's bar and discussed the moon's phases and the precise moments at which to plant and prune, I had my ha'p'orth of experience to add to their talk, and having found this tenuous link, I soldered it daily, getting to know people through our lunar speculations.

At the bar, Menchina was also under the spell of the moon's phases: her migraines were affected by them, her red bandanna was knotted to its cycle and the shifting winds. She assured me that not only did the moon affect her headaches, plants, cats, dogs and children, but it also affected pregnancies.

'Eh, *sì*, eh! All pregnancies tend to terminate around a full moon. With farm animals that's always, with women it's well known. "When the moon is full, a child is born." Both of mine clocked in right on the cusp.'

It was through the subject of the moon that we first became friends with Silvio the Poet. The poet (who was also the shoemaker) arrived at the bar every evening without fail at exactly eight-fifteen to drink his coffee and smoke two elegantly thin cigarettes. Unlike most of the local men of his generation (he was in his eighties), he dressed like a dandy in suits and waistcoats. His shock of white hair was immaculately cut and oiled, more like a teenager than the great-grandfather he was. The poet stood four foot nine inches tall at the high counter of the bar and only just reached up to it. He arrived one evening armed with a frayed piece of thick cardboard held under his arm like a bandmaster's baton. It was flaky, yellow and torn off a grocery box. It was also scrawled over in biro.

No sooner had he arrived at the bar than he announced, 'O Menchina, I have written a poem about the moon. I've been struggling with it all day. I feel as though it has throttled me and now my throat is dry – what shall I drink?'

Menchina kept a stock of proverbs which she produced like a Mediterranean Mrs Memory. Now she wouldn't have to frown and flounder to turn the talk to one of her pet phrases. Silvio's plea 'What shall I drink?' gave her the perfect opening for one of her favourites:

> *'Nun te mètte ntul cammino*
> *Si la bòcca n sa de vino.'*

(Never set out for anywhere unless your mouth tastes of wine.)

Silvio was a naturally abstemious man. He enjoyed wine only with his meals, as he promptly told us. His tipple, as we had observed, was a Martini served in a frosted glass with cocktail trimmings, but he would only sip at it, refusing all the offers of drinks he would be made during his stay at the bar. In his meticulous way, he demurred politely at Menchina's husky suggestion of wine, ordered his coffee and wet his lips with it. Then he turned to me abruptly and declared:

'I waited for you every afternoon last week. Why didn't you turn up as you promised?'

I had never exchanged more than well-meaning nods with Silvio and I told him so.

Menchina interrupted, 'He's deaf, you'll have to shout.'

He shook his head sadly after I had shouted, and smiled wryly.

'There's no badness in me,' he said. 'I'm a poet and my heart is in my rhymes, but another part of it worships women and their bodies . . . I love them, I always have. When I was a young man, I journeyed from villa to villa to measure ladies' feet so that I could come back to the village and make shoes for them (there were no shoe shops in those days, we *contadini* all wore clogs). I made a little mirror with a turning angle so I could measure a lady's foot and look up her skirt at the same time.

'Every year I grow flowers, a little patch of flowers to make bouquets. You promised to come and see my flowers and my poems and then you kept an old man waiting.'

Silvio's voice was querulous. Once again, Menchina interrupted.

'This is the *mother*, Silvio,' she shouted. 'You've been talking to the daughter before, this is the mother and her husband.'

Silvio looked startled and stared anxiously from Robbie to me and back again, measuring Robbie's height and frame and comparing them to his own miniature frailty. He apologized profusely, mostly to Robbie. He blushed and was generally flustered. As though to prove how serious he was at heart, he began to talk about the war and, finding me genuinely interested in his subject, he stayed and talked for an hour or more about Monte Cassino and the campaign that had led up to it. He talked about life in the village in the twenties and thirties while I shouted questions to him and translated the gist of what he was telling me to Robbie.

From that evening, Silvio the Poet never managed to distinguish me from the child Iseult again. I gleaned that he was asking the child to give him a photo of herself because he kept asking me by mistake, chiding me for my meanness in declining to humour an old man. The child Iseult refused to give him a photo, fearing to what use it might be put, but she complained of being cornered occasionally and bored half to death by his war stories.

The only person to establish a first-hand relationship with Silvio was Allie, who played cards with him regularly. The small boy and the old man harangued each other for hours about their hands and moves. In between, Silvio's tumbled memories poured out along with lines of his verse. Allie was our ambassador, he gave us safe conducts to the inner realms of the village, taking us beyond the hospitality and *bonhomie* into an area of friendship and obligation. Italy is a world of favours. Away from the highest echelons of bribery and corruption, the country and its towns and villages and individual families survive and thrive on a system of favours. It isn't what you pay that gets things done, it's who you know and what they owe you by way of loyalty.

Through Silvio, I came to know his nine children and, more gradually, his seventeen grandchildren, who were all grown up, some with families of their own. The Beauties were still trawling the *cantinas*. Robbie received invitations in their wake. It took him many days to recover from the ensuing acidity and pounding headache that this in-depth survey produced. I was gradually sifted out and escorted up into diverse kitchens to drink coffee and *mistrà* and to talk about ailments and children and recipes.

In Sant' Orsola there was a common pool of recipes and ingredients from which all the village cooks and kitchens drew. In an intensely regionalist country, with each region preferring its own cuisine to any other, I found this part of Umbria to be the most culinarily exclusive place I had ever come across. Many Orsolani, perhaps wisely, were suspicious of anything they had not personally seen either grown or raised. Most local kitchens were a curious mixture of the ancient and the hi-tech. Word had got out that at the villa we did not have a dishwasher. This, together with the absence of a chest freezer, was more disturbing to our neighbours than the, to our minds more pressing, absence of furniture. The two Marias urged me to get a dishwasher immediately.

'Washing-up is drudgery,' they told me. 'Eh, sì, eh! You must get a dishwasher, washing-up is a waste of precious time . . . time that could be spent doing something worthwhile, like making pasta.'

Three times a week, a wooden board one metre wide and one and a half metres long was set across each kitchen table. A narrow wooden rolling pin as long as the board and a series of specialized scrapers then joined it. A pile of flour was cupped out from a crock. The diehards used only stone-ground flour from one of the last local mills, believing that anything bought in a packet has been tampered with by the state and probably poisoned. A dip was made in the centre and fresh eggs were broken into it. Maria d'Imolo assured me that only fresh eggs were worth using, as the pasta would stick if any others were used. I have never dared find out if this is true. The types of pasta at the top of the Orsolano league table are *tagliatelle*, *pappardelle* (which are much wider strips, used to accompany game), *agnolotti* (wide-rimmed ravioli filled with ricotta cheese and spinach) and *cappelletti* (tricorn-hat shapes stuffed with three types of ground meat and spices). *Cappelletti* are for the New Year, and Christmas only. Pasta machines are scorned.

'You may as well buy the pasta in a fresh pasta shop if you're going to use a machine,' Maria d'Imolo told me many times. 'The machine compacts the dough and gives it a different texture and a different taste. It absorbs the sauce differently. You can tell it's machine-made *pastasciutta* instantly. It just isn't the same. Imolo isn't very *pastasciuttero*, he only really likes *tagliatelle*, otherwise I'd make it more.

'When we married, he said, "Can you make your own pasta?" I told him I never had. He shrugged and said,

"Well, you'll have to learn if you marry me. I can't eat that other stuff." It took me a long time to learn. I didn't pick it up as a child, like the other girls. I didn't grow up here, you see. I was born in the next village along. My father was a *contadino*. We were very poor then; all landless labourers were. To keep us going, my mother used to go to Milan to wet nurse. Each time one of my brothers or sisters was born, she would leave the baby with us at home and take off for Milan. There was a group of women from Sant' Orsola and from my village who did that. Sometimes we didn't see her for six months at a time.

'Well, Lisa, we had a neighbour who was, if you'll excuse the expression, like a piece of dog's turd that sticks to your shoe. He decided to make trouble, and he made trouble. He took my father to court on a trumped-up charge. My father had done nothing wrong, it was a neighbourly dispute but without any cause. Perhaps our neighbour couldn't bear to see a family growing up so well and happy.

'My father had to hire a lawyer. Imagine, in those days, to walk to Città di Castello and find a lawyer! It was all a terrifying process.

'He was acquitted, it was some stupid boundary dispute, but the lawyer's fees were more than my father could earn in a year in the fields.' Maria paused to shake her blonde curls in bewilderment at the existence of spite in the world at all. She looked quickly around her kitchen, at the giant television set in one corner and the stone fireplace carved by Imolo in his spare time, at her orderly ranks of gadgets and the plucked chicken hanging over the taps at her sink, and sighed happily at her lot, then sadly for that of her father.

'He had to go away, abroad. He went to Nice, and he worked his way out of the debt; sleeping rough and slaving. As soon as he could, he sent for us, his wife and six children. For the first two years we lived in someone's wine cellar, all eight of us, we lived hardly better than

113

beggars, but we worked. Then things got better. I lived in Nice until I married Imolo. He was back from Switzerland and I from France. As soon as we could, we came back here to Sant' Orsola. I wouldn't live anywhere else, and you know Imolo is like a bird denied the skies when he is away from the village. He doesn't even like to go to Castello.'

After her fourteen years in France, Maria seemed to have taken away with her only the language and a lingering fondness for a certain mushroom quiche and lemon-meringue pies.

'What about all the other French food, though – don't you like it?'

'Well, some of it, I suppose,' she said grudgingly. 'But it's not like the stuff we make here. When we were hungry, we would have eaten our aprons. I've eaten lots of French things, of course, but they're not like ours.' She shook her plump face and her curls. 'Life is a miserable business without any pasta.'

Maria was trying to teach me to make my own pasta. She was also very keen to train the Beauties in it, but had little success in luring them away from the *cantina*. The secret lay in the rolling and folding. The pasta had to be of an exact moisture or all was lost. If disaster struck and it wouldn't come right, the paper-thin yellow sheets of dough had to be dried out. To do this Maria used an electric hairdryer, running the hot air up and down the stubborn wafers of paste.

My own efforts were so abortive that I was relegated to the simplest of jobs during these pasta-making classes. I did some cutting, but even then under strict supervision as I didn't have a straight hand. I was told that it would take about fifteen years for me to get one. So sure-handed was Maria that, when the hour struck for *Beautiful* to be screened on the television, she would divide her attention between her perfect rendering of Umbrian cuisine and the erotic merry-go-round of her favourite soap opera.

Chapter 14

When the local police came up to the villa to investigate how and why one of the Beauties was in the local hospital having a shard of terracotta removed from her left eye, the conflicting stories were so baffling, and the witnesses' refusals to point the finger at a culprit were so stubborn, that eventually the case was dropped. Having been out at the time with Robbie and Allie, I never discovered myself why a game of cricket was being played in the passageway between the two parts of the house, or why a piece of terracotta was being used as a cricket ball. Because all those involved were friends of the Beauties, they too refused to say who had batted the offending chip. I did have a rudimentary grasp of what cricket was about, so I definitely had a head start over the puzzled *maresciallo* and his escort of police officers. In an area with very little crime, their keenness to press charges against someone was not easily thwarted, but what they managed to unravel was so surreal that it left them permanently suspicious of our menagerie.

Meanwhile, on the first floor of the local hospital, in a sweltering airless wing called Women's Medicine, one Irish Beauty endured the heat with a large patch bandaged over one eye, while her colleague sat beside her, urging her to make a speedy recovery so as not to miss the magic moments of the summer discos. On either side of them, and across the ward, local women sweated out their illnesses, battling with the added discomfort caused by streams of noisy visitors gathered around the wounded Beauty's bed. Our visits then were to be the first of many to that hospital, which we came to know so well that even now whenever I pass it, my feet turn automatically towards its cramped and savagely guarded reception lobby.

After five days of writhing in that most sanitary of saunas, one as an inmate, the other as a nursing companion, the Beauties returned, chastened, to the village. They celebrated their return by pooling their resources and buying a small blue moped, thus giving themselves the option of moving on from one distant night spot to another without having to wait for reluctant escorts. Once they had gained this new mobility and independence, we saw little of them again. They were supposed to stay until the beginning of October, but owing mostly to the irregular nature of our household (and, in part, to the endless fascination of the local entertainments) we had come to a relaxed arrangement, whereby their services were required only as custodians during our occasional absences, which left them to their own devices for the rest of the time. The downstairs flat kept up a busy social life of its own. Emergency deliveries of watermelons would occur at three o'clock in the morning, and the music blared out through its windows regardless of whether the girls were in residence or not. Many of their friends were also Iseult's, and many of their outings were shared.

The skeletal order I had tried to impose at the beginning had given way to a state of sporadic chaos interspersed with trips to Rome. When they were at home, as regularly as clockwork the engine of the tiny, battered blue *motorino* could be heard spluttering into action at ten o'clock sharp, counterpointed by the nightly argument as to which of the Beauties had to walk down to the bend in front of our neighbour Maria's house and which would get to ride the coughing chariot. The hill to the villa was too steep to take them both. In fact, the structure of an Italian moped is such that it was hard pressed to carry either of the strapping girls, but the brake cable burst without fail when they both mounted downhill. During the night, disturbing the owls and the nightingales and momentarily rousing us from our sleep, the girls returned, heralded by the stuttering minimotor of their steed at any time between 3 and 6 a.m.

The *festa* of the Madonnina del campo had been announced for weeks before it took place, yet the second summer festival of Sant' Orsola crept up and was upon us almost without warning. It was as if it was deemed to be so major an event that everyone, including ourselves, must know about it. Here was a *festa* that had been taking place for centuries. Originally, it was hosted by the confraternity of monks of Sant' Orsola. Each year, one villager would be appointed to gather in the food for the banquet. This meant going round the different monasteries and convents in the neighbourhood and collecting the flour, honey, eggs, meat and cheese needed for the feast. Local landlords all made donations. Now that the monks had gone, the *festa* was organized by the *proloco*, and the food was partly donated and partly bought.

The lunch was prepared in the kitchens and outdoor ovens of the sports field, and it was to this *campo sportivo* that Iseult and the Beauties led us one Sunday in July. Again the streets were scattered with broom petals, giving off a heady scent as the breeze blew them along. A procession led by the wizened Don Annibale made its way through the village, where hand-embroidered linen tablecloths and bedspreads hung from every window, white banners glaring in the sun. Two men carried the battered oil painting of Sant' Orsola putting the fear of God into the Saracens which I had noticed stuffed into a corner of the church during the earlier part of the year; behind them traipsed a group of acolytes in white surplices and brightly coloured sneakers, followed by a brass band and a snaking, sweating congregation of more villagers than I had ever seen before.

There was a general sloping away from the rear of this procession (which was making for the church) to go to the bar, and a growing exodus heading up towards the *campo sportivo* beyond and above the village, past the small walled cemetery bordered by cypress trees.

Over the three types of *crostini*, two types of pasta, roast veal with peas and groaning platters of roast chicken and lamb, we met dozens of new Orsolani. Our passports, as ever, were the children: Allie not only seemed to know everyone, but was in great demand to join their card schools. It seemed that during the early months he had not only mastered the game of *briscola* but was naturally lucky, and he was much in demand as a partner. The Beauties, in the spirit of the party, were called upon to demonstrate their considerable arm-wrestling skills, while Iseult was being booked up for the forthcoming dancing.

After an afternoon of dedicated drinking only slightly interrupted by sports, preparations began for the *ballo liscio*, the popular dancing that follows so many fêtes in Italy. An accordionist and an extremely drunken violinist took their places at the far end of a tennis court and as soon as they struck up their first tune, the Orsolani took to the tarmac. Imolo's wife, Maria, found herself there, gliding in the arms of Franco, a sixty-year-old builder who waltzed with the mechanical grace of a wind-up Victorian doll dancing over a mirror lake. Silvio, despite his eighty years and his apparent frailty, threw himself into the fray, seizing the biggest and bustiest of the women and girls. The cycle of tangos, waltzes and polkas was interrupted only by the occasional mazurka. Dusk fell, and the dance floor was packed. I had my feet crushed on a couple of polkas and stumbled through a waltz before retiring to the periphery with the conviction that I would have to take dancing lessons to master the steps. Two or three couples not only danced, but performed routines of the most magnificent complexity.

Long after midnight, we walked home, trudging the two miles back to our villa across the valley to the strains of the accordion and the hubbub of voices. It was as though we'd been baptized into the village by immersion, since we carried back with us on our clothes streaks of the slightly sour wine, stains of fizzy orange, splashes of coffee, grease from the late-night barbecue, mud, and patches of blood from a nosebleed Allie sustained on the football field. Long after we were in bed, the music played on, interrupted by shouts and cheers drifting through the night. We toyed with the idea of going back and joining in again, but the local wine is an acquired taste and it takes a prolonged apprenticeship to weather its effects. It had been all I could do to stagger home, my head reeling, while the drunken violinist, who'd looked when he started playing as though one sudden movement or, at best, another half-hour would have felled him, was still fiddling when we left, swaying precariously on his stool, his face growing redder and redder as he downed plastic cups of lethal brew. Next day, the girls all complained of feeling bruised from having so many small men bury their heads in their breasts as they danced.

After the second *festa*, there was a lull. Hoeing and watering had become the prime agricultural concerns. Water from the artificial lakes was pumped into the fields, keeping them green and growing at a phenomenal rate. In the woods along the wayside, wild plums ripened and fell, and the first apricots were maturing. The vines had groped and twisted their way across their wires, and the pollarded willow stumps that supported them were running riot, forcing out barriers of translucently green leaves and wiry tendrils. So many clusters of grapes had formed and were visibly swelling that it seemed impossible the vines could sustain such a weight. The last of the poppy seeds had been knocked to the ground by voracious wild chicory with its prickly leaves, angular stalks and ephemeral pale-blue flowers.

It was too hot for picnics any more. The fat in the salami and mortadella melted out of its meat and the bread curled up and threatened to toast as soon as it was taken out. But Allie was an indefatigable picnicker, and he continued to pack his wedges of dry bread and brown-paper packets of melting meats and tins of tepid sardines long after eating outdoors at lunchtime under a pounding sun had ceased to be a pleasure for the rest of us. It was the wild chicory that finally broke his resolve, together with a particularly hardy variety of thistle. This thistle could penetrate a canvas shoe, trousers, bags and anything we took to sit on, and its lacerating properties were savage. Reluctantly, Allie renounced his packed lunches out in the neighbouring fields for the simpler meals sprinkled with cement dust which was our daily fare.

At some point towards the end of July, the usual trappings of summer had expired, and almost overnight gave way to parched ferns and grasses, falling leaves, ripening blackberries and a palette of ochres, oranges and reds. As though by some prearranged signal, flowers died or burst on their stems, draining the colour from every garden. Well before mid-August, the summer as I had always known it seemed to be over. In scorching heat, all the usual transformations of the autumn were taking their toll. The leaves on the oak trees turned to a fairly uniform russet, but remained, shrivelled and crinkled yet doggedly stubborn as they clung to their trees. Most of the woods around the village were oakwoods: there were classic oaks, turkey oaks, a few holm oaks, and they all kept their leaves, not only until winter, but through it. The old leaves would be finally pushed away by the new ones, late in the following spring. Thus the landscape would never be entirely bleak; even in mid-winter the reds and oranges of the oakwoods would stay, thrown like a comforting, glowing veil over the hills.

August in Umbria was a sluggish month for everything except the tobacco and the Indian corn, which grew so rapidly that the dusty white roads that had divided the wide fields all year turned almost overnight into alleyways cut through the towering stalks. The tobacco was watered lavishly, and also sprayed at two-weekly intervals with some foul-smelling chemical product rumoured to have been banned years ago by both the EEC and the Government. During the relative cool of the evening, between slapping at mosquitoes and sipping wine, I gathered that the use of this product was a bone of contention. It was said to be carcinogenic, and many of the farmers who had worked for the few bigger local landlords in the past complained bitterly of its toxic effects:

'Even if you tie a handkerchief over your face first, it still makes you sick when you spray it. And it's no coincidence that there are so many instances of *il male brutto* (literally 'the ugly evil'), or cancer of the throat and stomach here.'

The days of August crawled slothfully forward. Allie was happy now that all the village children were on holiday from school. It gave him the chance to play football with them from morning till night. He seemed strangely unaffected by the heat, as did his new friends, scuffing around on a piece of wasteland and taking it in turns to burst each other's football. He had long since broken his vow to wait until the start of school to meet the local children, and had spent many sad hours squashing

Menchina's hibiscus tree as he clung to the railings of the bar to watch the comings and goings of the local boys.

Imolo had ensured his entry into the circle of anyone over the age of forty, and the child Iseult had found him a great many friends and allies by default in the age range from fifteen to twenty-five. But he still yearned to know and play with boys of his own age. We had met his best friend, Medium-sized Daniele, at Menchina's table-football game. Medium-sized Daniele lived next door and was addicted to mortadella sandwiches, which he ate at half-hourly intervals during all the hours of daylight. Never pausing in his munching, he had taken to watching our play. After a couple of weeks, he even volunteered to lay down his bread and take a turn in goal, where he proved to be ruthlessly skilful, deflecting the miniature balls from the feet of his two lines of defenders.

He told us proudly that his father was the best table-football player in Sant' Orsola. He began to wait for us in the evenings to join in our games. He organized a match with another team of players, and one day he asked Allie to play with him, and called him Allie. From that moment, he and Medium-sized Daniele became inseparable. If anyone dared to mention that Daniele was on the plump side, let alone fat, Allie leapt to his defence with such passion that the name of Medium-sized Daniele was devised and stuck. It became Allie's ambition to invite Medium-sized Daniele to our house. Imolo advised him to wait until the furniture arrived. Thus the joys of camping began to pall even for Allie.

Meanwhile, the battle for our impounded furniture had reached a standstill. Our three forty-foot containers were still caught in a bureaucratic mesh at Livorno. There had been a dock strike at Genoa some months previously, and this had delayed all shipments to Italy, including, specifically, our own. In the ensuing chaos the containers had been held for so long that the documentation covering their eventual release was out of date. Documents all have a life span in Italy and, unlike the average Italian, they die young.

Because there had been a strike – an unforeseen event – the Port Authorities at Livorno refused to take any responsibility for this state of affairs. I tried in vain to convey that while appreciating their innocence in the matter, I wished to stress my own. The containers of furniture were caught in a black hole which was not covered by any of the tens of thousands of by-laws and clauses and sub-clauses so dear to any Port Authority, and we were threatened with never seeing our property again. To a background of arguing and screamed greetings, I hugged the mouthpiece of the one public telephone and tried to reason with the shipping agency and a certain customs official to allow our goods through. Our conversations had reached a point where the shipping agent would invariably end up saying, with infuriating and patronizing calm, 'Now, I know you don't like this, Signora Santowbin, but I'm going to hang up on you again.'

Outside Regina's bar, I then settled down on one of the long benches to wait for a double Vecchia Romagna while the children dismantled the ice-cream freezer in search of Blobs, Super Marios, Boomies or whatever gaudy ice lolly they happened to be addicted to that week. Robbie drank beer of a tepid and unappetizing variety beloved by the locals during their bowling championships in the long sandpit behind the bar room. He reminded me of all the hurdles I had overcome to get our first container of furniture out of Norfolk and into Italy, out of Livorno and down a Venetian canal. He urged me to go and talk to them in person. I pointed out that they were refusing to see me.

'Well, we're camping here – take the children and go and camp there until they give you our things.'

★

Having no car that could legally take us all to Livorno, I enrolled the services of one of the taxi-drivers from Città di Castello to ferry us from Sant' Orsola to the port. When I booked the taxi, it was the driver who suggested that we travel on August 10th, *il giorno delle stelle cadente*, or the day of falling stars. He explained that on August 10th and then only, if you see a falling star and wish on it, your wish will come true. In the absence of falling stars, but surrounded by a great deal of falling masonry, the child Iseult, Allie and I set out on that day with its lucky aura.

We were all psychologically prepared to plead our case in the most helpless and heart-rending fashion. The five-hour taxi ride, the heat and the eventual cost combined to produce a convincingly pathetic effect. I had warned the children to be silently tearful and to leave the talking to me. I had warned them to show no surprise, no matter what tales I spun. Their tears had to flow freely but there was to be no unseemly noise. We all had to look our most endearing and be scrupulously clean.

Although we had set out in that state, by the time we reached Livorno we were all smudged and damp with heat. We cleaned ourselves up in the back of the taxi with a box of babywipes, a clean pressed frock for the child of a modest nature with a monstrously starched white collar, a dazzlingly white sailor suit for Allie, and a teasingly demure suit for myself. We were parked next to the goods refugee camp by the port, where I had been told our impounded furniture was to be held indefinitely and at my expense.

When we started to wash in his car, the taxi-driver looked decidedly unhappy and opened his door. When we started to change, he got out and walked about, intermittently pretending not to know us and returning to remonstrate.

'What are you doing? What are you doing in my car? What will people think?' he implored and ranted.

The goods compound was deserted, and we completed

our toilet without paying him any attention except to apologize and assure him that all would be well. When we emerged, a miracle of good housekeeping, he was impressed and wished us a half-hopeful '*Auguri*' as we made our way to the office buildings.

After thousands of years of sexual inequality, it seemed only fair to be able to fight dirty over this matter. Paradoxically, the dirty bit entailed presenting a clean family of the kind any Italian man would be proud to go home to and protect. One of the few advantages Italian bureaucracy has over other kinds is that there is always a bottom layer of something genuinely human and giving. Approached the wrong way, this layer instantly turns, like quick-setting Superglue, into an invincible barrier, but approached tactically, it can be flexible enough to allow a solution.

At Livorno, it took us an hour to find the right office within the maze of the port building. It then took under ten minutes to state our case (with a few omissions and embellishments), ask for our relevant documents to be stamped and achieve the release of our furniture. No money changed hands, and no personal services were either offered or asked. Allie had coughed discreetly on cue as I described how he slept on the bare floor. The child had brushed the tears away from her lovely eyes, and I had used my most deferential manner as I spoke of my invalid husband and my inability (as a mere woman) to cope with the Italian legal system. The previously intransigent official, with whom I had argued many dozens of times on the telephone, suddenly saw that we were decent people. We spoke and wept in a calm, reasonable way, and he responded by doing the reasonable thing and letting us out of his labyrinth of officialdom. The furniture would be with us in two days' time.

The next few days were bliss. Not only could we think of the reunion with all our things and the comfort in store for us, but also while we were away in Livorno, Robbie had found another lake. This was not a jumped-up pond, it was a proper lake, hundreds of metres long and hiding in the woods beyond our house. It was hidden from the *palazzo* and the village in both summer and winter. It was approached by an avenue of cypress tress and was only three minutes' walk from us. This new lake, encircled by oaks, willows and Scots pines had a seductive stillness. Dragonflies hovered around the edges where branches dipped into its unruffled waters. At one end, there was a band of meadow between the shore and the trees. A tangle of purple vetch stretched over it like a raised veil. At the other end, a smooth flat rock sloped over the edge, making a perfect deck for sunbathing, fishing or contemplation.

To Allie's delight, we reintroduced our picnic lunches, taking a basket of provisions and a tablecloth down to the lake and keeping the heat at bay by swimming in its deep cool waters. When we quizzed Imolo as to why he had never mentioned this new and beautiful lake, he responded with bewilderment, in true Umbrian form,

'But what would you want with two lakes? Giovanni's lake was good enough to wash in, the other one is only water.'

It appalled him that we swam in the lake and he feared so for Allie's life that I had to replace his armbands with a fully fledged life jacket.

'It isn't natural for people to swim,' Imolo insisted. 'The good Lord didn't give us fins for a good reason.'

His views were shared by the entire village, who all knew about the new lake but never dreamt of venturing into it.

'It's twenty-two metres deep,' they told us. 'It isn't safe.' Anything to do with water that was over the height of an average bathtub was considered not only unsafe but unhealthy. Meanwhile, we all swam and wallowed in our new find and its perfect seclusion.

*

Each meadow around the *palazzo*, slotted into the surrounding woods and the irregular patches of vineyards, was like an inexpert painter's canvas, covered with splodges of colour. There had been first a mass of pale-blue speedwells and then a rash of scarlet pimpernels, giving way quite suddenly to dandelions and then buttercups, poppies and scabious in rapid succession. One colour wiped out the next as though nature had changed its mind, cancelled a pigment and sent in another. Mid-May had been a time for entire fields of puce wild gladioli, June was scarlet with poppies. July specialized in wild orchids, hundreds of them nestling in the tasselled grass. By mid-August, these orchids had died in the heat, even the rarest, the five-foot-tall lizard orchid with its bizarre reptilian flowers.

The fields and waysides had been blue with speedwells when we arrived and they had turned blue again with the startling celestial blue of wild chicory. We tramped through its knee-high flowers in the rubble of our garden, we brushed through it on our way to the lake, crushing peppermint leaves underfoot as we went, leaving an aromatic trail all the way down to the water.

Imolo and his workmen were laying the pink travertine marble floor of the entrance hall, a present from Robbie's mother, and he seemed momentarily less interested in my company than he had before. The housepainter came up every day and wrought his own colour miracles on the walls of the rooms on the first floor. The promised two days of final waiting for our furniture came and went and nothing remotely resembling a container lorry raised the dust of our road.

When I telephoned, the customs official did not hang up on me, neither did he shout. He called me '*cara signora*' and assured me that the lorries were on their way. This turned out to be not strictly true. They did not arrive until two days after *ferragosto*.

Chapter 15

August 15th is always a holiday in Italy: Ferragosto. It is a time when, traditionally, the Italians divide into two factions, those who try to escape the heat by fleeing to the mountains, and those who try to escape the heat by fleeing to the sea. It is a time when the entire country grinds to a halt and takes its holidays; shops, bars, offices and restaurants a barricade their doors and stick up little notices, torn from a child's exercise book and written in spiky italics, 'Chiuso per ferragosto', as though the sight of the bleak, battened façades could leave anyone in any doubt. I think of Ferragosto as being like a race, as indeed do many Italians. The holiday begins as though at the firing of a starting pistol, and a tremendous traffic jam takes to the roads single-mindedly. It would be possible for some to leave a day early, and others a day late, but there is magic in the numerology of Ferragosto and a demented belief in safety in numbers.

In Sant' Orsola, there is a fear which amounts almost to a superstition about leaving the village. A handful of families make snail tracks towards the sea at Fano, and some of the young people set off in groups for trips to the Lakes or to famous cities. Few go abroad, as those who have tried it have come back with horror stories about the food. Even travellers to Nice pack their cars with enough supplies to see them through until they can get back to their own kitchens. On the whole, Ferragosto for the Orsolani tends to be a time for the men to wear shorts and silly cloth sunhats, to sit around the bar, to do odd jobs on their own houses and to read about the endless traffic queues elsewhere in the *Cronaca Umbra*.

It's a bad time to be born or to die, a bad time to get ill or need a lawyer. Everything is at a standstill. It was a bad time to be waiting for anything to arrive.

Every afternoon, a pair of buzzards glided over the valley, swooping and circling from the ridge of hill behind the villa to the far crest of Sant'Agnese with its dark regimental poplars standing out against the skyline. Robbie and I were both armchair falconers; we dreamt of keeping our own Harris hawks and a buzzard or two. We drew up plans for an ornate falconry with carved wood weatherings, and we made yet more lists of all the accoutrements to buy, one day, in the unforeseeable future when everything was complete.

On a more realistic note, we had kept all our potential visitors at bay until such time as the furniture should arrive. Having been given a green light at Livorno, we telephoned friends and family all over Europe to announce that we were now officially at home. Our first guest to rally to the call was Fidoe from Bristol and we named the finest of our future guest bedrooms after him to mark his arrival. Being one of the most meticulous men I have ever met, he still has nightmares about the cement dust that enveloped him during the entire duration of his stay.

Our second guests came from Holland, unprepared for an adventure holiday, but they proved themselves to be eminently adaptable and slipped into our regime of lake, laziness, lunch, building works, bars and long evenings under the stars with such ease that they stayed far longer than they had originally planned.

Our fourth visitor was my sister, Lali, who lay in the sun until her entire body had turned an alarming shade of red which she had to nurse with calamine lotion for the best part of a fortnight. There was competition at the villa over sun tans; it had been the Beauties' sub-tropical tans that had induced my sister to suffer her burns. The Beauties were already the colour of teak after hours of diligent exposure, but they were determined to reach shades of mahogany unknown in the Emerald Isle so as to impress their friends back home. They sacrificed themselves on a daily basis on a blanket in a small patch of meadow above the garden. The child Iseult and our Dutch guests sun-worshipped with them. My sister watched enviously from the scorching safety of her room.

Allie prowled through the undergrowth of brambles and goose grass and iron girders, searching for lost footballs. It was he who alerted the girls to the groups of spectators who had gathered a little higher up the hill and who, fully clothed and further draped in bushes, sacrificed themselves to the heat in order to spy.

One of the peeping Toms was invited down to talk and share their warm Coca-Cola on condition that he sent away the others. I noticed that the Beauties, who had been keen to master Italian, and the child, who was anxious to perfect it, had all gleaned extraordinarily comprehensive vocabularies. From inside the big kitchen as I mustered the lunch, I heard them hurling abuse at the voyeurs, blending the local dialect with stock Italian obscenities in defence of their right to lie naked in the wild chicory.

Our fifth guest arrived with the containers of furniture and threatened to take up permanent residence. Whatever trauma or surprise our first guests may have felt upon discovering both the loveliness of our new house and its disconcertingly wrecked and empty interior, it can have been nothing to our shock on realizing just how much furniture and building materials, how many doors, bathtubs, papers, books, manuscripts, canvases, carpets and junk can be professionally packed into a forty-foot container. When all three of them arrived together, they had to be unpacked. Imolo and the workmen promptly enlisted every able-bodied person in the house to help. Not all of them were able-bodied by the time the six pianos had been lugged upstairs, together with the seventeen wardrobes, twenty mahogany chests of drawers, the brass beds and all the other heavy Victorian paraphernalia.

After seven hours of forming a human chain, lifting and carrying, lugging and groaning, we all assembled at Regina's bar and sat slumped on her benches as exhausted as any of the usual chorus line waiting to be called into the opera that gathered there. Imolo sat looking down the valley with the eye of a mystic, drunk with fatigue. He held his squat glass of wine firmly in his hand, emphasizing the missing joint in his right middle finger. Gigi's blond crew-cut and matted, naturally white eyebrows were always further highlighted by dust by the end of the day, but that night they were also draped with vestigial cobwebs. Then there was Verniccio, with his face taken from a Greek tragedy: half-handsome and half-scarred by an oil burn. He flexed his biceps as a kind of side show before drifting in to join the young blades at the bar. Verniccio had carried hundreds of pieces of furniture up the stairs. Leonardo with his curly locks and Pre-Raphaelite face was so tired he looked in shock.

Our household sat silently watching the fields, and the awkward arrival of Pietro the last Castellano. Long before he reached Regina's bar, he began to converse with Gigi (Pietro regularly chose the person furthest away from him to talk to). His voice carried across the field of low ridges divided by rows of corn. He was called the last Castellano because he was the last person to be born in the twelfth-century tower on the hill behind Sant' Orsola's second church. This tower, once reputed to have been as high as the imposing watchtower of Città di Castello, was brought to its knees by the earthquake of 1917 which cause such havoc in the area. By the time Pietro was born there it was a four-storey affair, now reduced to three and derelict.

Pietro was rarely seen without a baseball cap perched precariously in his greying curls. He was gaunt, and his very pale blue, protruding eyes had a mischievous light in them. He had the manner of a vaudeville turn, swaggering with his hands on his skinny hips, tapping his nose conspiratorially before shouting out some secret.

As the evening began to spread its tendrils across the valley, cooling the air and dulling the glare, we began to recover. Pietro couldn't decide whether to side with the women returning from the fields or the workmen on our bench. The women had been hoeing weeds, and were making their weary way back home clinging to the tractors for a ride up the hill or along the road to their old stone cottages or their new breeze-block houses. They had hardly the energy to smile; instead, they gave a side shake of their hands to intimate the punishment they had received that day in the fields. They did not even reply to the ribald comments shouted out as their dusty convoy rumbled by.

Pietro the last Castellano was shaking his head, jerking his shoulders from side to side. He did not return with the women, neither did he feel broken enough by the day to join the row of fatigued, stunned men on their bench. Inside, the young men had ceased the noisy numbers game they had been screaming out. They sat down for a couple of minutes to swill down some cold water or iced orange fizz (believed by many to be a general restorative). The blades were soon up again, chafing and organizing and arguing with an energy that Pietro could no longer either match or muster. So he hovered at the edge of the ditch on the far side of the narrow track alongside Regina's bar.

I had been too tired to notice earlier, but Brendan, the driver of one of the container lorries, had not left when the other drivers did, but was sitting next to Imolo, staring out into the middle distance with him. I remembered that he had been anxious to use a telephone. He showed no signs of having done so. Seeing me look at him, Brendan responded by producing a large bowie knife with a string handle and a viciously serrated edge.

'D'you know what this is for, then?' he demanded, running the blade delicately over his tiny fingers.

'No,' I said, wondering why his small yellow eyes had lit up quite so intensely.

'It's for sawing through human bones. You know like, if anyone was to mess with Brendan, he wouldn't hesitate to give them grief with this.'

During the unloading of the containers, Brendan had declared himself too exhausted by the trip to assist in anything as distressing as manual labour. So he became the self-appointed director, standing in the way of everyone else as they struggled with the weighty furniture, telling them how to lift, carry and heave without himself damaging a muscle. Brendan was five foot three, if that, and walked with the mincing steps of a would-be Nijinsky. His frizzy orange hair stood out as though he had suffered a series of severe shocks. There were tufts at many different angles electrified into place. Despite the sweltering heat, he never removed his denim jacket, although he spoke frequently of the terrifying muscles that rippled under its sleeves.

Taking the back flap of the first container as his soap box, he had told us more about his life than anyone really wanted to know, particularly at that time of unloading. Brendan was an aesthete, a worshipper of the body beautiful. There was nothing immediately beautiful about his own misshapen miniature body, but he told us that his anatomy was loved deeply and well.

'No one gets near to Brendan.' It was one of Brendan's many eccentricities to refer to himself only in the third person. 'He has tuned every nerve and muscle of his body like a Stradivarius.'

By the time we were on our second container, with twenty men, the Beauties and me borne down by fatigue, Brendan, perched on the ledge once more, informed us that his passions in life were martial arts and the theatre.

'Brendan has played in theatres all over Europe.'

The more we worked, the more excited he became, frothing slightly as he enunciated to an increasingly irritated workforce a list of all the foods, drinks, habits and countries that drove him 'spare': 'And when Brendan goes spare, that is not a pretty sight.'

Brendan's diatribes were mostly ignored, but Imolo, who could not understand a word of what he said, was fascinated by his impersonation of a prancing hobgoblin and his frenzied oratory.

'Who is he? Where does he come from? Are there a lot of people like him in your country? Why doesn't he help? He should take his jacket off, he's shaking sweat on to the upholstery. He doesn't look like a well man to me. He's going to have a seizure if he doesn't shut up. I'm going to have a seizure if he doesn't shut up.' And so on.

At Regina's bar, Imolo watched Brendan caressing his bowie knife with the same interest he reserved for the antics of a rare insect discovered in the course of his work.

'How come this one has stayed on when the others have left?' he asked me.

'I don't know,' I told him.

'Is he staying long?'

'I don't know. He said he wanted to make a phone call.'

Brendan did eventually make his call. Then he said he hoped he would not be inconveniencing us if he stayed for supper, there was apparently some hitch with his next job.

He stayed for supper, which in his case was scrambled eggs and spring water because he told us he never ate anything else and he wasn't going to start trusting foreign concoctions at this stage in his training. After supper, he said that he would sleep in his lorry and leave at dawn. His empty container was blocking the main entrance to the villa. There was something both pathetic and menacing about Brendan.

Next morning, we all woke in the comfort of proper beds to the chorus of birdsong mixed with the war cries of Brendan as he practised his solitary martial arts in the rubble, wearing his denim jacket and a pair of orange tights over his spindly legs. A half-circle of astonished workmen stood around him, watching him lunge and thrust with two bamboo canes he had found among the lilies.

For two days, we and our shattered guests nursed the aches and strains of the unloading and were all too tired to appreciate fully that Brendan had come to stay. The tyres on his huge lorry were mysteriously down on one side. Brendan felt as strongly about the lorry, it seemed, as he did about his own unviolated body. He allowed no one to approach it with an eye to jacking it up and putting any spare tyres on.

The child Iseult, who apart from Brendan himself had suffered the least exertion during the unloading (having only deigned to carry two bundles of coat hangers up the stairs and then taken to her mattress on the pretext of total exhaustion), had the benefit of most of his company. On day three, she called a junta and told us what we already knew: Brendan was an arch fantasist and not necessarily a safe one.

On day four, I overrode Brendan's insistence that no one touch his vehicle, and, with Imolo's help, we called in the local garage. The lorry, at least, was now roadworthy, but Brendan still showed no signs of going. Hints, suggestions and ultimatums slid off his back.

Our guests had been suggesting getting out to see some of the spectacular surrounding hill towns, to escape the tight web we had woven around Sant' Orsola. On the first night of each visit, the famed hill towns would be named and proposed as places to go: Gubbio, Assisi, Montefalco, Spoleto, Santa Maria Tiburina and the old Etruscan capital of Perugia. All of them were relatively near.

'These places are practically on your doorstep. They're famed the world over – you've got to go. How come you've waited so long?' we were chided, but I found it too hard to explain the sudden quenching of our wanderlust, or the relief at finding a place to sink our roots, and our continuing amazement at all we had to see and learn within the microworld of Sant' Orsola and its immediate environs.

Within walking distance of our house there were three ancient towers: one, eleventh-century and linked to the Knights Templar, sat across the vineyard behind the villa and filled many waking fantasies as I gazed towards it from my ruined loggia. The other two were twelfth-century, Pietro the last Castellano's birthplace and another on a hillock behind the bar. Between them, they formed a triangle of defence. The Etruscans, Romans, barbarians and Tuscans had all been through our valley.

The last occupation, after a gap of nearly seven hundred years, took place during the Second World War. For centuries Sant' Orsola had been a forgotten place, useful only for the wood from its outlying forests and the indifferent pickings of its laborious agricultural arrangements. In the middle of the thirteenth century, its present hamlets were conquered by the Signor Marchese Guido di Monte Santa Maria and became part of the numerous possessions of the ancient city of Città di Castello. Subsequent battles were all to be with the elements and with diseases, either of its inhabitants or its meagre crops.

One by one, our visitors found themselves drawn into the lazy enchantment of our own unsung little bit of Umbria. Trips away to the surrounding cities were continually postponed, replaced by forays to the village, the lake, and up into the hills that rose to the crest of Zeno Poggio, from where the sunsets bathed the pockets of scorched meadow in the most lovely of lights.

In my guise of inept amateur historian and bumbling social anthropologist, I burrowed into the ways of the village and its past through the memories of our neighbours. Cenci, Beppe del Gallo, the Signora Maria, Gelsomino the blacksmith and Menchina took it upon themselves to be my guides.

History here is something that is buried under every rock and boulder. Farmers ploughing their land unearth it, and ancient peasant women crouched over their bread ovens know it. And daily reminders are flaunted in stone. The churches, *palazzos*, villas and farms testify to the extraordinary history, culture and art of the Italian past. Umbria is no exception, and neither is Sant' Orsola. There is so much to know and remember that the local *contadini* have re-invented a version of its truth, like a landscape by numbers. Certain main points stand out and are added to another event, which is added to another with little regard for the spaces between.

The Renaissance master, Luca Signorelli, is believed to have fallen in love with a girl in the hilltop village of Muccignano *en route* to work at Santa Maria Tiburina. It is known that he paused in the neighbourhood. He is a part of the history. It would then seem that at some time in the eighteenth century, a scion of the Nicasi family, who were the lords of this manor, was attacked on his way to Cortona. He returned and died shortly afterwards. His son was taken in by an uncle. This child then lost most of his inheritance in ways that are only hinted at. What is sure is that the stone arch that joined the upper and the lower roads of the village, once linking two Nicasi villas, was stripped of its covering gold leaf and nothing is left but a stump of stone on one side. Beyond what was once that golden archway, according to both Cenci and Menchina – apart from *La Nona*, a mysterious sleeping sickness that ravaged Italy in the 1890s, and the earthquake of 1917 – not much took place in the intervening years.

On closer inquiry, I learnt that the fields were planted with corn and strips of other crops, from flax to pulses. There was poverty but little hunger. The crops were gathered with little gain to the *contadini* who gathered them. The *mezzadria* system of sharecropping was generally used. The landlord provided seed and land, the peasant worked, and then they split the profit. The split was not half and half as the word implies, but 60:40 in favour of the landlord, and all costs returned. On poor soil, this led to a lot of poor families. There was general agreement that the Church had abused its privileges and stripped from many families those few possessions that they had.

There was also general agreement that from 1916 until the end of the Great War, an ox-drawn convoy dragged the wives and widows of soldiers at the front into Città di Castello to draw their war pensions. This convoy of women had remained very much a part of popular myth. Their antics escalated over evenings soaked in wine. In the towns and walled cities, there are more specific accounts; people are aware of key points in their history in a more conventional way. In the country, there is a blur: a misty night sky lit only by bright stars. The *contadini* find their way through the past, guided from one light to the next. As in all small communities, history has dwindled or swollen at the whim of the teller. There is a gossip factor built into its facts. A story is told and repeated, honed and retold, altered imperceptibly and handed on. Lines are forgotten and replaced at random. Names merge and fade, dates are vague and always linked, as by a guy rope, to something else. There are befores and afters. Before the earthquake ... after the war ... Very few stories actually concur. Individual memory has used its process of selection.

As a writer, I found myself overwhelmed by the wealth of material given to me every day, its stock increasing and mounting as surely as the hoards of food and wine stored in every *cantina*. The seven years that I had spent living in the Venezuelan Andes on a sugar plantation in a scattered community that existed in a time warp, isolated from the rest of the world, had been the essence of my writing and a most privileged springboard for my imagination. The place itself, and the fifty-two families of peasant workers who lived there with me, had marked and moulded me, for good and for ill, into what I am today. I was drawn into that claustrophobic world, initiated into its secrets, enriched by the original and archaic use of its high Spanish, by my long and enforced contact with the peasants and their endlessly extended families. The child Iseult and I were both branded by the elements of sub-tropical fantasy that ran through every aspect of our life there. I left Venezuela and the hacienda fleeing an impossible and violent marriage. Subsequently, I never missed the violence or the madness of those Andean foothills, but I did miss the sense of community, the closeness and the mystery and the myths. I also missed the harmony of rural life, of being harnessed to the land and the elements.

It was in Venezuela that my dream of a big house first came to fruition. The Spanish colonial mansion that I'd lived in there was called quite simply *la Casa Grande* (the Big House). Like the Villa Orsola, it too had been empty. I used to roam through its halls and corridors, terraces and towers, in a bemused state of dream fulfilment. During my early years there, more and more children from the outlying parts of the hacienda came to visit me and stayed. They too were struck by a nightly restlessness, moving constantly from one room to the next with their sleeping mats and woven slippers and their plastic bowls of soap suds, into which soiled underclothes were hurled and left. I never fully learnt the geography of the Big House, not because it was actually so very big, but because the household grew and shrank, decamped and hid from day to day.

In the early days most of the girls (whom my mother-in-law referred to grandly as my maids) were under the age of six. They lived in a world of continual exploration, inventing games, stuffing leaves down the lavatory bowls they had never seen before, tearing foliage off the shrubs in my garden, teasing the small zoo which had somehow accumulated around me, and playing hide and seek. Each of these small maids had a nominal job which they were called upon to fulfil once a week. Thinking back to those days of my first marriage, I can no longer recall all the chores of all the children who lived with me in the Casa Grande. I know that Alba, from the age of six, took it upon herself, through some gruesome predilection, to be the killer of chickens. These she despatched on Thursdays with a flat stone and a single blow to the neck. Her four-year-old sister picked flowers for me, and learnt how to arrange them. Another, Adriano, chopped parsley for my fourteen beagle hounds. The others have faded into unconnected names and faces.

I was always too much of an outsider on the hacienda ever to really fit in. I was little more than a child myself when I arrived, and I made friends of the children and took them in, initially to nurse them through illnesses that their parents had neither the time, knowhow or money to defeat. My years as an invalid had taught me a smattering of nursing skills, the rest were gleaned there in the field. When the children recovered, they stayed with me, ferrying food and clothes back home to the wattle and daub huts where their mothers struggled to bring up a dozen children at a time. The children warded off my loneliness. My point of contact with the adults of the estate was as their boss and therefore, in that semi-feudal society, I was doomed to be socially out of bounds beyond the ritual formalities. I found a way to be close to them by gathering their stories, and they to me by telling and retelling them.

From that time, I suppose, I had been searching for another lost valley surrounded by hills where a tight community would take me in. My intervening years of obsessive wandering, trailing my own children from train to train, had been a part of that search. In Sant' Orsola, I found by chance just such a community, with the added boon of a collective memory. And it was a far gentler place. There were no stabbings here or outbreaks of diphtheria. There were no feuds or midnight vendettas. The dust track to our house needed for rain, but not to wash bloodstains away. The cruelty and the violence of the hacienda and its extreme poverty had been replaced by a pride and pleasure that were far easier to live with.

The advent of visitors brought back memories of the hacienda. I felt my house full of people and my hands full of their care, and I was contented in a way that had long escaped me. The presence of Imolo and his team in our house didn't really disturb me. I was confident that the day would come when he would move out, and meanwhile we were growing close with a closeness that had been denied me in the Andes.

The only blot was the continuing presence of Brendan, the lorry driver and martial arts expert, whose daily proximity was causing not only friction but fear. The human saw was very much in evidence. Dozens of tea chests of kitchen equipment had been unpacked, yet never fast enough to keep abreast of his penchant for scrambled eggs. Pots, pans, frying pans and cake tins mounted by the sink, all encrusted with the remains of his frequent snacks. His looks grew wilder and his speeches more bizarre.

Eventually, all other guests and family convened in Robbie's attic studio to hold a meeting. The studio's bareness had been replaced by an exotic mix of furniture and ornaments. There was a chemist's cabinet full of jars of Florentine pigments, and *chaises longues*, velvet drapes, Turkish rugs, easels and paintings. Our council of war was held in luxury and interrupted only by the swooping martins circling in and out of the window frames.

We decided that since Brendan would not leave, we would. This would be our opportunity to explore the neighbouring hill towns. We would leave *en masse*. We called up Imolo and explained the plan to him. Despite having been more than concerned by Brendan's lengthening stay, he thought the plan was madness and said so in no uncertain terms. We told him he had to lay off work the next day, a Friday, and if Brendan was still there on Monday morning, he was to stay away for a day or two.

'He'll steal everything you've got.'

We reminded him that the stuff had arrived in three containers, and Brendan only had one.

'He'll fill it and then what will you do?'

We explained that Brendan had shown himself no friend to carrying. It is easier to unload than load a forty-foot container. It seemed that Brendan liked our company; if we left, with luck he would too.

'Why don't you call the police?' Imolo said. But none of us wanted to do that. So a bowl of eggs was left in the big kitchen together with a note to say that we had all been called away and didn't know when we might be returning. Then we took our leave of Brendan, who was doing high kicks in the downstairs loggia in a blue leotard and his denim jacket, and we set off on a sightseeing tour of Umbria.

Chapter 16

Our first stop was Città di Castello, from where Fidoe was planning to catch a train on the Umbrian state railway line that dawdled to Perugia. There he could get a connection to Rome and catch his flight home. He left the legacy of his room and took with him, despite his best efforts, a startling tan. We said our farewells. The Beauties were also on their way to Rome, where they had made many friends.

I had grown fond of Città di Castello because of its buildings and its narrow stone alleys and its cups of what looked like purple mud but was actually an exquisite version of hot chocolate. After our unpromising start there, my few subsequent visits had all contained an element of trauma. Caught up as I was in the world of Sant' Orsola, cushioned by the local *geometra* who kindly handled all the paperwork that might otherwise have driven me mad, I went there only when forced to by the unpleasant necessity of visiting our bank.

Even when I was a small child, my mother was inordinately proud of my literacy, and always somewhat more reticent about my blatant innumeracy. The simple skills of addition and subtraction eluded me. Added to this flaw was the precarious state of our finances, the massive expenditure on the house, and the Italian system of making all cheques out to oneself to be passed on anonymously from person to person, from the north to the south of Italy and back again and not cashed for anything up to a year, thus rendering a simple current account a nightmare. Negotiations with my and Robbie's agents were conducted via the telephone at Regina's bar. The local post seemed to involve the use of donkeys at several stages of its passage, delaying letters by anything up to five weeks. None of these factors made for easy banking.

The Sienese claim to have invented banking in the fifteenth century. The first bank was the Monte dei Paschii di Siena. Banks are still major employers in Italy, with exams rather like the old Civil Service's to select the lucky thousands who will join their arcane business. Strings are pulled and cousins wheeled out to help shoehorn aspiring candidates into their mystical ranks. Few of the system's modern methods have percolated through either to Siena or to its less illustrious branches. A medieval air of mystery prevails, an autumnal gathering of leaves of paper and unbroken cyphers in partitioned palaces. It took a lot of getting used to, and required much study and care to survive. Since these hadn't seemed to be viable options in my case, it required a great deal of good luck, some charm and a vivid imagination. Baffled by figures, and intimidated by the small print of my numerous banking contracts which all offered years of penury and prison, I sometimes had no choice but to smooth the troubled waters of our current account in person.

Imolo showed me how to avoid contact with the bank by cashing cheques at Menchina's shop. However, from time to time, on receipt of awesome telemessages that somehow found their way up to the villa with far more ease than any of our other post, I had no choice but to go to Città di Castello.

Banks in Italy are guarded by armed guards who try to

look as inconspicuous as possible in a country where bank robberies abound. An electronic button on the outer, bullet-proof door gave entry to a glass cubicle. The next electronic door would not open until the first had closed. An illustrated label told me that in the event of a robbery, the safe would timelock for 144 hours. Nothing opened if the button was pressed by anything other than naked flesh: a glove or bandage sent the alarms squealing. Once inside, difficulties were taken into a little labyrinth of cupboard-like offices at the back. I always found myself waiting there as I used to wait outside my headmistress's study at school. Banks, schools and doctors all give me a sense of being in disgrace. Dante could have done wonders with the tortuous meanderings inside my bank. Whenever I escaped once more into the sunlight and the grey cobbled streets, I headed for the *caffè* across the main square, light with the sense of reprieve.

The general consensus of opinion as we set off for Città di Castello was that there had to be more to it than a hospital, a taxi rank, a great hot chocolate and a dreadful bank. Outside the city wall, beyond a double row of horse chestnut trees, old men were playing *bocce* with heavy clay balls, and a lorry was selling pigeons and guinea fowl to a queue of haggling women. Our Dutch friends had come armed with a guide book which listed Città di Castello as occupying 'the site of Tifernum. In the Middle Ages it gave employment to Raphael, Signorelli, Vasari and the della Robbia ... The Duomo is by Elia di Bartolommeo ... in the treasury is a silver altar-front presented by Celentini II (1143) and the treasury of Canoscio (5–6C) ...'

In Sant' Orsola, whenever anyone was digging, and some-one else asked them what they were digging for, the answer would be, '*il tesoro di Canoscio*'. It was Imolo who explained this treasure to me. It had been hidden in the ground in the ninth century to protect it from pillage.

After the Second World War — in the fifties or sixties, Imolo wasn't sure — a local farmer had been preparing a new strip of land, turning it from stony scrub into a useable field. He had been working on it with his tractor for some days when he discovered two big flat black dishes encrusted with earth. These he took home and filled with chickenfeed in the yard outside his farmhouse. Years later, a pilgrim on his way to the Sanctuary of Canoscio and the shrine of the Madonna delle Grazie lost his way. Seeing the small farmstead, he paused to ask directions and to drink some water. Calling and finding no one at home, he went round to the back of the house to see if anyone was there. A dog barked on its chain, and chickens and ducks were the only other living things he saw. The latter were drinking from a muddy basin into which an outside tap was slowly dripping. Drawn by thirst, the pilgrim went to investigate. He stooped to drink, and on turning off the water, his eye was drawn to a crude pattern engraved in the edge of the dirty water dish. Rubbing away some of the grime, he realized that the dish was silver.

Thus, I was told, began the fabled excavation of the treasure of Canoscio. Guided by the farmer, archaeologists unearthed a complete trove of ninth-century ecclesiastical silver. There were large plates and small plates, chalices of various sizes, spoons, salvers — everything, in fact, used by a priest at that time in his church. Every neighbourhood has its tale of hidden treasure. It is the poor man's dream. When the ground is either so parched or so frozen that digging it becomes a trial, I think these tales begin; luring people to superhuman efforts in search of gold. When I first heard the Canoscio story, I was inclined to believe it because of its absence of any gold: silver is less mythical. There in Città di Castello I felt absurdly pleased to discover that the treasure of Canoscio really existed, for it lent credence to all Imolo's other stories.

After the cathedral and its museum, we found a trattoria in a side street that served fresh *gnocchi* with *porcini* mushrooms and cream, and ate a lingering lunch there. Then we sat on stone benches under the shade of ancient plane trees and tried to eat ice-creams while the sun competed to melt them in our hands, in a public garden bounded by the city wall. Beyond it stretched crumpled green hills streaked with woodlands.

As we sat admiring the view, Allie and the child Iseult discussed in Italian whether we should go to Perugia or Assisi next. A middle-aged lady who was knitting with a large sleeping child in a pushchair beside her was following their discussion. She had cropped, greying hair and a wide face with a businesslike, no-nonsense smile.

'Go to both of them,' she interrupted, 'see them both.'

'We're going to, we just can't decide which one to see first.'

'Believe me, it doesn't matter if you're seeing them both. You shouldn't argue. It doesn't matter where you go, as long as you don't go to Gubbio.'

At that moment, there was a lull in our conversation and the lady took centre stage. She rose to the occasion, smiling slyly and raising her hands in mock despair. I felt obliged to enquire further.

'Don't you know,' she said, 'the Eugubini are mad. All of them. Never marry an Eugubino, everyone knows that.'

'Mad in what sense?'

'In all the senses. They're just mad. Have you never seen the *ceri*?'

Candles? I had seen plenty of candles; in fact the upper realm of our house was still lit by them after dark. So I repeated, '*Ceri* . . . yes.'

'Eh, but have you seen the *ceri* of Gubbio?'

I shook my head.

'Well, if you'd ever seen them race them at their *festa*

you wouldn't have any doubts about their lack of sanity. They do it on May 15th every year, and they have done for nearly a thousand years. And such a rigmarole! They have three massive candles carved out of wood, one for each quarter of Gubbio. There are three quarters . . . typical Eugubino logic, eh? Three quarters make a whole!' The lady was enjoying her audience and getting into her subject with undisguised relish.

'My father was custodian of a villa there for ten years, I spent some of my childhood around Gubbio, so I know it a bit. Nobody knows it well . . . not even the Eugubini. They're a muddle of twine you never get to the end of.

'Well, there is a story that Gubbio was the site of a Roman lunatic asylum, and anyone in the Empire who was mad was sent there, and that loads of them stayed and intermarried and that's where the madness comes from. The Eugubini themselves deny this. I've never heard a single one admit to the Roman asylum, but everyone else says so. Ask anyone; it's well known. Nobody is sure whether the asylum was in the city or whether the entire city was like an open clinic.'

The child in the pushchair stirred and demanded, in perfectly formed Italian, a dummy and a bottle. These were promptly produced from a plastic bag on the back of the pushchair. The child shifted in the cramped seat and settled back to sleep.

'The Eugubini say "Run three times round the well" – you know, the fountain below the ducal palace – three times and then you are one of them: mad as a hatter.'

An hour later, we were there, in Gubbio, making our way through its Porta degli Ortacci to the steep road that clambers up through the pale-grey stone of its streets to the polished grey stone of its medieval *palazzos*. The numerous shops seemed to sell antiques or local majolica, or antiques and majolica. There was a glut of jars and jugs, for which I was a willing customer, buying a chemist's jar in brown and blue to use in the kitchen, and a jug for flowers.

Gubbio cast a spell on me, it took my brain and addled it with its loveliness. For hours, until nightfall, I made my way through the maze of stone alleyways, treading the different levels, running up and down the hundreds of wide and narrow steps linking the parallel streets that hug the contours of the steep hill of Gubbio. I grew heady with the wealth of sights and pictures, churches and frescos, and the magnificent vertiginous views sweeping across the rooftops of the nestling city and out across the plains at its feet and the mountains beyond them. I was too excited by the city to take in properly the extraordinary Palazzo dei Consoli towering majestically over everything. I leant against the cold stone of the balustrade between the Piazza della Signoria and the view falling away and found myself memorizing the floor of that main square lying in herring-boned obeisance at its feet.

Even before I had seen the interiors of any of the vast grey *palazzos* or the cathedral or any of the churches, or the works by Sinibaldo, Palmerucci or Nelli, I was in love again. It was Gubbio as a whole that smote me, more than any particular building or painting or view. I fell for the place and its overall sense of antiquity and the strange enclosed feeling of self-possession. The shops, bars and restaurants were mostly open, the people were not. It was as though they all shared a secret too important to tell and too time-consuming to allow them to mingle with mere visitors.

In between my moments of Eugubino reverie, I was aware of Allie and Iseult running up and down the grey steps, weaving in and out of alleyways and in and out of bars, tanking up with Coca-Cola and ice lollies. The others had divided up, taken their separate ways through that labyrinth of palaces and past power. I had decided to return, often, to Gubbio, to take in the details. Meanwhile, I felt drunk with just being there while dusk descended through the gaps of stone. Leaning against the balustrade over the precipitous drop from the Piazza della Signoria, I learnt (through my bad habit of listening to other people's conversations) that according to our local newspaper, *Cronaca Umbra*, Gubbio has the highest suicide rate in Italy. From two American tourists, I gleaned that a prehistoric meteorite had fallen just outside what is now the city of Gubbio; and that there was a theory that the dust it raised was responsible for the dying out of the dinosaurs. From a group of boy scouts I learned that Gubbio lights up annually to become the biggest Christmas tree in the world. And from the child Iseult I learned that three of the five *caffès* she had visited with her brother were a rip-off, but she had gone again before telling me which was which.

It was late when we reached Assisi that night; too late to expect to find hotel rooms for us all. Despite that, we were lucky and we did. The night was fragmented by bells. We were used to this from Venice and they failed to disturb our sleep. We ate our breakfast on a terrace looking down over a pink and beige street, in that city of pale-pink and beige travertine marble. There was a smell of coffee and hot buns and, from somewhere, a whiff of jasmine. The pastel colours of Assisi's stones were taken up by the skirting hill covered in the pale grey-greens of olive trees.

There was a gentleness about the place: even the sunlight had a soothing quality as we picked our way uphill towards the Basilica of San Francesco. We spent the best part of two days there in the Basilica, putting 100 lire coins into the lighting slots the better to marvel at Giotto's frescos of the life of Saint Francis. Allie acted as our coin runner, procuring change in return for a small fee. Such is the beauty of the church and its muted colours, its vaults and steps and arches, that we could have stayed for months and never tired. But it was still the aftermath of the Ferragosto fortnight scrum, and although the crowds were no doubt smaller than they might have been a few days earlier, Assisi was still a place of pilgrimage and we were by no means the only pilgrims.

Our friends departed for their long drive home, dropping the children off at Perugia station on their way. Robbie and I took the silver Panther back to its dusty parking place outside the Villa Sant' Orsola, picking the children up at Città di Castello from the station in the new suburbs beyond the city wall. We were too squashed to see anything until we had unfolded our legs from the car, but as soon as we had, we noticed with relief that Brendan's container had gone.

Chapter 17

We were in the doghouse with Imolo, who was shocked at our having abandoned the villa. From the beginning, we had lived in search of his praise. He had never been out of sorts with us before for more than a few minutes. Robbie went out of his way to regain his approval. Imolo wore beige overalls bought at Nunzia's emporium in the village, so Robbie did too. He even took to wearing big work-man's lace-up boots until he discovered that the local variety weighed so much he could hardly move his feet, let alone run up and down four flights of stairs several times a day. The children were exonerated from Imolo's disfavour: they could do no wrong in his lapis lazuli eyes.

By the end of the week, Robbie, too, was pardoned and became once more the pet maestro. Imolo sought him out in the stratosphere of his studio to watch him stretch a canvas while he came out with spontaneous affirmations such as, '*Bravo, Maestro*' every time another few nails were hammered in.

Downstairs, traipsing round after Imolo, watching his work, I was unstinting in my praise, at which he smiled sheepishly. Like a small child, he loved to be watched over. Despite this, and even though he lavished compliments on the others, he refused so stubbornly to admire anything I did that I came to admire him for his consistency. It was a game we played. No matter what I did, in his teasing way, the fact that I had done it automatically made it wrong. If I filled a bucket with water, then it was badly filled. If I planted a shrub, it was badly planted. If I fed the cats, they were badly fed. If I bought a nail, it was useless. If I filled in a form, it was wrong, if I cooked a meal, it had to be tasteless. And if Robbie and I made a mistake (such as abandoning our lovely villa to a stranger with a human saw, taking his precious Allie away in the process), then most of the responsibility for that bad decision must have been mine.

It would have been easy to dismiss Imolo's criticisms had he not been like a peasant version of Leonardo da Vinci's Renaissance man. He seemed to be versed in limitless fields of practical knowledge. For all his gruff denials, his aura of kindness was such that his reluctance to encourage me seemed somehow utterly justifiable, and feelings of inadequacy blossomed in the rubble and the weeds. Robbie had found a way through the carapace with his painting and also with his lifting skills. When we had unloaded the container and Robbie had shifted heavy furniture by himself, Imolo had kept calling out, '*Bravo, Maestro!*' While I merely played into his hands, hauling weight around and getting stuck and needing to be rescued.

The pact was sealed when a crucial piece of terracotta fell from the scaffolding platform. It was a heavily decorated pediment for the first-floor architrave. It was irreplaceable and it was heavy, and Robbie was standing underneath it. The boy who had inadvertently knocked it over squealed. Imolo called down, '*Attenzione, Maestro!*'

Robbie, even with his still minimal grasp of Italian, caught the tone of urgency in Imolo's voice and, by reflex, caught the falling piece. The workmen were overcome with admiration. Imolo from an unscaffolded window on the second floor shouted down his respects.

'*Complimenti, Maestro. Bravo!*'

Meanwhile, Robbie concentrated on keeping his lunch down and staying upright as he beat a dignified retreat into the ground-floor ghetto to be bound and treated for a severely dislocated wrist and a wrenched shoulder.

Having thus gained some approval for the adult side of the family on Imolo's own ground, neither of us could bring ourselves to admit to Robbie's injuries having occurred as they did. Alas, this led to an erroneous reputation for strength. Every time an ultra-heavy load had to be carried, Imolo said, 'Wait, get the Maestro, he's really strong, remember that falling terracotta, eh, call him.'

The reluctant hero had set himself on the road to a hernia, but like the roads of the local processions, it was, at least, scattered with petals.

Behind Imolo's back, I continued to go to great pains to persuade my miserable runner beans to do their bit. I had planted them late, and they flowered late, and the few stunted beans they produced were out of season. The lilies flowered and perished in the heat after a week of remarkably fine blooming. The morning glories were still flourishing and so too, against all the odds, were my seven secret tomato plants. Living up to all Imolo's verdicts of ineptitude, I refused to stop scrabbling around in the caked dirt of the vegetable patch, trying to coax both rocket and lettuces to grow. I waited until Imolo had knocked off work to water them all, dragging a hose pipe round the house. The hose was hot and so was the first gush of water that spurted from it. It didn't quite reach the furthest of the vegetables, so I smuggled out buckets of water to them and scraped little trenches through from one hidden plant to the next.

All the vegetable gardens looked identical in the village; they were all prepared, manured and planted on synchronized days. Imolo had offered to bring up a tractor in the autumn to prepare our soil when he prepared his. He didn't believe in doing things by halves. I knew he would have disapproved of my 'wasting my time' planting anything in the wasteland of my vegetable plot until the appointed time for its ploughing.

The lilies had proved my best allies. Imolo deemed their blossoms to be freaks and their apparent health to be sheer luck, but I knew that it would have taken more than luck to get flowers of that quality to grow in such near-total neglect were there not something very special about the garden after all. I had been able to take a bunch of them to Maria and Imolo to take to the cemetery. I had been able to wallow in Maria's praise and to notice the genuine surprise on Imolo's face. Our two Dutch friends had also been impressed by them and had offered to provide me with as many more bulbs as I wanted, to see if lilies might be the solution to a problem which had begun to needle me.

Under the apathy caused by the heat, and the feeling of well-being induced by the atmosphere of the village, and my happiness at having found my dreamhouse, I had a nagging fear that something was about to spoil our plans. The more I talked with the local farmers and the more I learnt of their crop yields and profits, their ways and their means, the more it seemed to me that tobacco was a serious problem. Not only did its noxious sprays intoxicate the valley, killing any birds and animals rash enough to go near the treated plants, but the heavy watering then washed the pollutant substances into the river, killing the fish that once thrived there, and further contaminating the land. Strictly speaking, we were geographically above this. Imolo admitted the problem, but advised me to leave well alone.

'What can you do about it?' he said, and went on to explain that, to make matters worse, the labour-intensive tobacco crops that had once made Umbria rich were now proving too arduous to produce in an age when such crippling drudgery was no longer undertaken lightly. A new crop was needed, but who would ever have the initiative to try one? Sant' Orsola was an area where nothing changed, on principle. No one was going to vary their crops or the plants in their gardens. No one was prepared to risk change, for it was seen as the harbinger of disaster. There was safety only in the parameters of their known world, and ever since the turn of the century, their known world had included tobacco. The plants were reared in green houses covered with plastic sheeting whose skeletons punctuated the fields every few miles, resembling in summer the ribcages of beached whales, with the last bits of plastic adhering to the bowed frames flapping like the vestiges of whitened flesh. For as long as anyone could remember, the fields had been full of tobacco plants and the village peppered with tobacco-drying towers with their rows of tin chimneys. The lake, our lake, was enlarged seventy years ago to irrigate the tobacco.

Maria d'Imolo told me how, as a child, she had helped thread the tobacco leaves on to long strings in the summer evenings.

'The women helped bring in the harvest, then they cooked, and in the evenings it was their job to thread the leaves together ready for drying. I never worked as hard as the others, I was just a child, but I always remember those days and the closeness I felt there, listening to their stories and learning their songs. I used to dream of it when I lived in Nice. Of course it's different now, the harvests are more mechanized . . . but the picking is still done by hand. It has to be, machines can't choose like we can.'

Children still assisted in the fields. School here was a half-day shift, it was over by half-past twelve. Since the tobacco tended to be grown by family units, even very young children helped as best they could, planting, weeding and picking alongside their parents. The children all laid aside their designer clothes to don the regulation rags of the tobacco fields. They earned good money for their toil. Allie harboured a new ambition to drudge in the fields alongside them. He plagued Imolo about how much money he could earn per hour, per day, per summer.

Tobacco used to be heavily subsidized. Farmers with as little as four acres of tobacco had been making enough money each year to live very well. The work was intensive from April to October, then they rested for the remainder of the year. I could have talked myself to exhaustion about the evils of the sprays, as many of their detractors had done before me. It was the reduction of the subsidy on tobacco which had really induced the crisis. Without the extra money, the tobacco planters and their co-operatives were not earning enough to make it worthwhile. Everything began to point towards further reductions in the tobacco subsidy. By the time we arrived, many of the fields that had been planted with tobacco the previous year had been turned over to the old Indian corn and a few to capsicum peppers and sunflowers, the traditional poor relations of tobacco. But these are crops that grow better elsewhere, and their market price is low. Four acres of Indian corn will scarcely keep three dogs in food for a year. It became clear that an alternative crop would have to be found; something that could use the labour-intensive skills of the villagers and be grown for a high market price on relatively small plots of land. Maybe lilies would be the answer.

I began to dream of fields of lilies all around the villa, and to fantasize about farming again myself after a fifteen-year gap. We had only six acres of land, including the plot the house was built on and a small wood. But just one acre of lilies would mean hundreds of thousands of flowers. Sensing imminent competition on such a massive scale, even my straggling morning glories rallied and began to bloom. I realized that the time wasn't right to divulge my plan to Imolo. It was a far-fetched idea and one that would be bound to be met with derision. To broach it now seemed to be asking for trouble. Instead, I began to order bulbs, to gather information, to get our soil analysed and to contact some of the top flower growers in Holland (thanks to our Dutch friends) to see if anyone would be willing to assist me with technical advice on such an apparently hare-brained project.

Time seemed set aside to absorb the soothing cycles of the hills and watch the blackberries ripen in the hedgerows and butterflies congregating on the luscious nettles. It didn't really seem like the time for the Beauties to have an accident on their *motorino*; but they did. The local hospital, divested now of its mystery, was virtually deserted and severely understaffed. Every airless corridor seemed to breathe apathy along its trodden marble floor. Once again, one girl lay in bed while the other leafed listlessly through a pile of magazines, nursing her. This time, the injury was to a leg. The damaged knee had been stitched in the small hours shortly after the accident, but an infection later set in and the swollen limb had to be treated more seriously. For weeks after they came back to the villa the wound refused to heal. This may have had something to do with the heat, and it may have had something to do with the injured Beauty limping stiff-legged down the hill at all hours of the night in search of a disco.

On several occasions, as I lay in bed considering my lilies, I could hear the pathetic whimpering of the wounded girl protesting noisily at being dragged out to keep her friend company. They would scramble down the steep slope through the cypresses outside our bedroom window and then stop on the dirt road below. After a great deal of bargaining, wheedling, bartering and bribery, they would then progress slowly down the hill, leaving a sad trail of groans behind them.

As the house filled with visitors again, all vying for bedroom space with the bats and housemartins, we began to feel as though we had always lived at Sant' Orsola. Our plans to return to Venice in September became more and more vague and were gradually lost in a wave of local protest. Surely we had come to stay, Imolo asked at regular intervals. Why had we undergone such discomfort merely for a summer house? After a few glasses of wine, Imolo would call me outside and walk me briskly up and down the parched forecourt, telling me tearfully,

'Lisa! You can't take Allie away from here. It would be a terrible thing to do. He loves it here, he's one of us, he's like family. He'll pine.

'Do you think we would have worked like this if we'd known you were going away? This is a labour of love. I know we get . . . well, we will get, wages, but we're doing this for you, for all of you, for Allie.'

At the best of times, to look into Imolo's eyes was to feel a sadness so intense, he seemed to be carrying all the world's troubles on his strong shoulders. To see Imolo with tears in his eyes was heartbreaking. For several weeks, we walked the corridors in a mutually tearful state.

At the beginning of September, I discovered that one of the reasons why I was so prone to being tired and emotional was because I was expecting another child.

We didn't make a conscious decision not to go back to Venice, we just stayed on in Umbria, tying knots and making friends and dropping roots into the rocky subsoil.

But our debts were getting out of hand, and the bank at Città di Castello turned nasty. We borrowed money at inflationary rates and faced the fact that I would not be able to write my way out of our dilemma. I have never been able to combine pregnancy and prose.

The new wave of guests included the film director who had for years been trying to make a film out of one of my novels and in the process had become a friend. He took up a vigil at the half-sized snooker table, taking on all comers. Robbie's and his oldest friend, Paddy the Irishman, also arrived and merged into the landscape and the masonry. Sometimes, in the afternoon, in defiance of the blistering sun, a crude form of cricket was played outside. We never had enough visitors to make up proper teams, but they played three and four aside, and argued endlessly about whose turn it was to dive into the sloping brambles and retrieve the ball that had inevitably landed in their depths.

The Beauties began to make preparations for their departure. Allie was getting ready for school. He had been duly registered and a folder of documents – vaccination certificates, duplicate birth certificates, papers to prove where he lived and who he lived with – had all been presented to the relevant authorities. Because of his adoration of Medium-sized Daniele, who already attended the same school, he was far less nervous than he might have been. Medium-sized Daniele had given him a list of all the accessories he would need for school and a list of the kit required to join the local junior football team. For the latter, the traditional strip of shorts, shirt, socks and boots was the least part of the luggage. Every boy had to arrive armed with a hairdryer, gel, a bathrobe, slippers, shampoo and a comb. They emerged from their matches as a brigade of aspiring Valentinos.

We continued to frequent both Regina's bar and the second bar. Long after the need to use Regina's telephone had passed and our own telephone had been installed at the villa, we kept going down to the strange pantomime of Regina's for old time's sake and to play *bocce* in the lumpy sandpit there.

Our conversations were often repetitive, consisting of question and answer sessions. The information solicited was always the same, drawn out, doubted and asked for again. The locals found it hard to believe that anyone in their right mind would want to tackle the *palazzo*. Nobody had really done so since the middle of the First World War. No one had made any real progress since the turn of the century. Would it ever be finished? Was it true that there were three hundred and sixty-five windows and doors, one for every day of the year? Was it true that there were rooms no one had ever been in? Was it true that if you fell over the edge of the stairwell, you'd die? Was it true . . .

These questions, so often repeated across the length and breadth of the valley, were from people who knew the house better than we did but who wanted to hear these things from us to make us, I supposed, a part of their community by linking our voices, if nothing else, to their myths.

The main question, though, was never so much what we were doing there, or even who we were, as always did we like it? Did we like Sant' Orsola? Did we appreciate what a uniquely decent place we had chosen to settle in? Our first affirmatives had been hopeful civilities. Then, as the months merged into each other, demarcated by the crops and the village rituals, we began to realize how fortunate we had been to stumble on such a closed and yet such an open society.

It was in September that work commenced on the fitting of the windows and shutters of the first floor. Once they were in, this first floor would be complete (save for its doors). The chandeliers were in place, the telephone was connected in the big kitchen, with the child semi-permanently grafted to its receiver. The rooms were furnished and elegant, having swallowed up all our treasures yet still leaving a feeling of space. The upper long corridor had not benefited from the work and time given to the lower one, so although one couldn't actually fall through it, it took some careful stepping to hit the right boards and not send little trails of debris down to the floor below. The main bedrooms, on a good day, with all their furniture and their rugs and carpets, looked quite impressive with their rows of windows facing out to the west, north and east respectively. It was here that our guests had settled in. The top floor (the third) was still all Robbie's studio. Then, over the ballroom, there was another big but lower room, covering the same floor area, which we called the billiard room, because in our dreams that was what it would be some day.

The more people who came to the villa to stay, the more confusing the arrangement of rooms seemed to be, so we named them all in an attempt to make things easier. Alas, this was not the case, since the labels reflected either what the room might be in the future, or the name of the first guest to stay there. It was easy enough for us to identify and locate Fidoe's room, or the Venetian room, or the Arab room, or the Blue bedroom, but a lot harder for visitors to know that a certain plastered box would eventually be painted blue, or another featureless space one day have Venetian-style frescos and drapes, and yet another, a tented Arab ceiling. However these confusions were trifling. Hunt the bathroom was a more time-consuming game and one that not everyone mastered.

Luckily, no one fell out of any of the gaping window holes, or down the stairwell, or through a floor, despite a few valiant efforts in that direction, most noticeably by the three-year-old son of my best friend who'd come out from London to convalesce after an operation. The divisions within the house made it very relaxing, as a rule: entire families could spend time there without getting in each other's way.

Often, we'd only meet up in the evenings over dinner (cooked by me, but making full use of all the local fresh ingredients we were being indoctrinated to rely on). I've always liked cooking. I started as a child, growing up in London with my mother and sisters with a great deal of time on my hands. My mother used to come home tired from work and ravenously hungry, while I had either been lying around legitimately languishing with glandular TB, or else was feeling guilty for having played truant yet again from the smart girls' school in Dulwich my mother was so proud to have sent me to. So I started to mess around in the kitchen, and eventually out of the messes some decent meals began to emerge.

Later, living communally in Oxford, and then in Italy as an adolescent bride, I was galled to be told what a bad cook I was by one of my first husband's friends. This wasn't something he just mentioned in passing, it was an insult that he repeated every three days, whenever it was my turn to cook on the rota. During the very dead hours of every afternoon that I spent on the sugar plantation in Venezuela, surrounded by my giggling minions, I turned my hand to cooking with obsessive zeal. I used to cook for at least twenty people a day there, sometimes with help and often without, but most of my victims were the children and peasant workers from the hacienda. They quickly rebelled against any fancy ideas I might have had about cuisine, so I learnt to be quick and simple with a few special dishes up my sleeve. Cooking in Umbria for our summer guests reminded me of those Venezuelan days.

I was also reminded of how much I like to live communally, provided I have enough space to find solitude. Occasionally, the communality took on bizarre proportions and the household seemed to resemble a chaotic ship. Every time there was a storm, which was on average about every two weeks, it would be action stations. Summer storms in Umbria are sudden and violent. From the beginning of August the workforce had dropped to just Imolo and his mate Gigi, and after Ferragosto, not even them. Even when they had been there, it had seemed better to cope with our storms alone, since Imolo never helped us shift our furniture out of the path of the driving rain without trying to persuade us to store it away and live without it until such time as the rooms were ready and the windows made. Alternatively, he would suggest that we all go and live in the bits of the house that were more or less habitable. We felt that if we did this, the bedrooms would never be finished. They had been empty for so long that it seemed easy to imagine them staying that way. There was an allure about the sheer abandonment of the villa. Since, technically, we had more than enough rooms already restored in which to live, there would be no necessity to go forward.

There had been what amounted to a drought all summer. The farmers were desperate for rain. The vineyards were suffering, the crops were suffering, and the land was scorched. When the rain came, it did so with a vengeance. There was no more warning than a roll of thunder across the azure sky and a sudden blast of wind. Then the sky turned grey in blotches, as though a quantity of black ink had been spilt across it, and drops of rain the size of peas began to fall.

Within minutes, the thunder had blown itself up into recurring explosions, followed by bolts of lightning cracking into the surrounding woods. The first time it happened, we rushed to get our books, rugs, drinks and hats out of the garden and to cover the cars with their convertible tops. By the time we got inside, the villa was awash with rainwater driven in by the wind along the east façade. The big kitchen was a shallow pond bobbing with detritus. The flowers had blown out of their vases, papers and letters were soaking into the puddles and the window shutters were crashing against their frames, caught in the cross-currents. The morning room, dining room, writing room and study beyond, all had their shutters and windows banging, and the dining-room carpet was an oozing sponge. There was panic while the mahogany furniture was moved out of range. Every raindrop left a pale water mark on it. By the time we got upstairs, the beds, mattresses, rugs and books were all thoroughly soaked.

Half an hour later the storm was over, and by teatime no trace of it could be seen in the garden as people returned to sunbathe in the late afternoon rays. It took another day to dry out our things. After that, it was red alert at the merest hint of rain, with everyone racing upstairs to gather in their belongings, batten down windows and, where there were none, to pile up all the furniture on the far sides of the rooms. We became adept at rolling carpets and lifting them on to chairs or beds. We developed a routine that had to last all winter.

After the first storm, rain followed regularly every five or six days. These were not showers: the rain was torrential inside and out. Where the stretch of roof was still missing over the stairwell, waterfalls occurred. Downstairs, in the long alleyway, we resorted to the Venetian custom of laying duckboards. One day, the floor level would be raised a foot; meanwhile, the existing cement floor sank under a foot of water.

When it rained at night, an added hazard were the power cuts that regularly accompanied any change in the weather. The village was prone to power failures. We were, perhaps, the least affected of all the villagers, having grown so used to darkness in our early months. Imolo was an expert on power cuts. They caused him endless delay and irritations since they interfered with his tools. From the first week, when he had got the electricity company to run a working line up from the Signora Maria's to power his drills and the cement mixer, the power cuts had interrupted his work. Every time the lights went, someone had to go all the way down to the Beauties' flat and re-activate the trip switch in the meter box. This was an unpopular task and one we drew straws for.

Imolo could tell what other people were doing in the village by the strength and availability of our electricity supply. Sometimes he would say, 'Get on with it!'

'On with what?'

'That's the football team using their hairdryers after a match.' Or he'd say, 'Someone's forgotten to stagger their dishwasher today.' Or, 'There are too many ham-slicers going together this morning.'

Someone who was never disturbed by power cuts, storms or any of the other intermittent plagues at Sant' Orsola, was the Scotsman who came to spend a month with us and our hazardous nascent cricket pitch. He rose at dawn and, with the single-mindedness of an officer conducting a crucial campaign, he requisitioned whatever he needed for the day's play from the debris scattered around the garden. He tore down the fencing around the vegetable garden to make his nets, extending it with sheets of the thick wire mesh that Imolo used to reinforce concrete floors. He purloined girders and doors, shutters and planks, and made a miniature shanty town of the forecourt. He paced out a pitch diagonally and then improved it, removing rocks and boulders, levelling the rubble with a garden rake, cutting down thistles and generally turning the ground into his own personal playground.

As other members of the household rose, he conscripted them into helping him. When I complained about my Portuguese pink marble fountain being right in the middle of his pitch and therefore a target to be broken before it was ever mounted, he strapped a double mattress over it and worked on. Allie, Robbie, the child and the Beauties all found themselves batting, bowling or fielding for him – although, as an impartial observer, it seemed to me that the batting fell almost exclusively to Robbie and his Scottish friend. Visitors and delivery men were all in danger of being press-ganged into the field. Standing six foot six and with his skin burnt shocking pink by the sun, with a mane of silver hair and a T-shirt bathed in perspiration, he was not an easy man to deny.

Had potential players needed merely to deal with the Scotsman, I think some of them might have chosen to read or sunbathe; but there was also the Brigadier to contend with. The Brigadier, as the Scotsman's companion Miss Myrna explained, was a retired Indian Army officer who had never mentally left either India or the officers' mess and who sometimes manifested himself. He was both cantankerous and senile. He arrived one morning at breakfast, springing out of the Scotsman's mouth in a way so commanding that half the assembled company jumped. He stayed for several weeks, never once ceasing to be the Scotsman's *alter ego*. The first time Imolo heard the Scotsman being the Brigadier, he eyed him up as though measuring him for a straitjacket, and then accepted him philosophically as he had done with other, less obstreperous guests. However, he did find a pretext to bring Maria up to the villa to behold him.

'Is he an actor?' Maria asked.

I shook my head. 'No, he's a journalist.'

'Eh, *bé*!' she said, and took to coming up each day to watch his antics from the safe distance of the big kitchen as he sweated in the wicket.

Chapter 18

All the signs of the summer had disappeared, except for the heat, which had embedded itself in the soil, in the bark of the trees, in the fence posts on the road, in the water of the lake, in the roof tiles of the villa, in the demijohns of wine in what had become the toolroom and general dump on the ground floor. The heat had eaten its way into the newly varnished wooden shutters and begun to peel off films of paint. It had driven the half-wild cats into the cool of ditches. It had ripened the peaches on their trees and the plums, and dried the last of the ungathered fruit into shrivelled skins.

September was a lazy month for me. I spent more of my days pottering around the garden, plotting and planning future beauties, and less time with Imolo and the men, who were back at work after the August break. They had moved up to Robbie's studio and the roof, driving the Maestro down to the room that was destined to be my studio on the first floor. I had no need of a study for a while, I was studying my thoughts, becoming increasingly introverted. I was wrapped up in my pregnancy, which was moving towards its third month, and in monitoring the changes of each new day brought to the autumnal landscape around me, emblazoned by the sun.

Allie started school and drew me temporarily out of my

reverie. The school was a pale-ochre building by the church. There were fourteen children, divided into three classes; three teachers; and an attendant whose role I never managed to work out. Allie had bought an unbelievably gaudy rucksack, on Medium-sized Daniele's advice, and he had practised staggering around the villa under its prodigious weight, ballasted with coffee-table edition school books.

Maria d'Imolo came up on his first day of term to help prepare him for the forthcoming ordeal. She personally packed his fluorescent rainbow rucksack with his new pencils, ruler, seven exercise books, each with a gaudy cover, the leaden books, his individually wrapped cake and the small carton of pear juice without which no Italian mother feels safe to let her child go to school. He looked so scrubbed and brushed and starched that I hardly recognized him. His long golden ringlets were plastered back against his head and he looked pale and nervous as the white school minibus careered up our drive and screeched to a halt beside the resident bulldozer.

He returned at twenty to one, radiant and very full of himself. He was going to like school in Sant' Orsola. He had liked the five other schools and nursery school he had so far attended, but it had been hard for him to overcome his shyness. Now he was confident, reeling off the names of new friends, anxious to get back down to the village to play with them.

The days of relative calm that fell to me at the house were contagious, and the child Iseult retired to a hammock out of range and earshot of the lingering cricket games. She kept a stack of books on one side of her and a row of Coca-Cola bottles on the other. For much of her time, she made lists, which then got left around and drifted across the garden and the neighbouring fields. They all began with austere resolutions, such as: 'Get up, do twenty press-ups, swim in lake, drink eight glasses of spring water with freshly squeezed lemon juice. Breakfast half a grapefruit, lunch ricotta cheese, spinach salad, no dressing. Dinner grilled fish, salad. Facepacks, massage, improve my mind, learn French . . .' When she tired of the lists, she drank the Coca-Cola, feeling healthy and virtuous. She tired early of the sportsfield and was deaf to the commands of the Brigadier. When the stumps mysteriously went missing, she relented and got Silvio the Poet to whittle new stumps for her and also two bails.

One day, she brought Silvio back with her, escorted by two of his daughters and a thin man with a stutter who seemed to be no relation. Silvio had decided to introduce us to the arcane secrets of his special walnut liqueur (*nocino*). He chose to impart this news through the medium of his friend, who, on account of his stutter, took the best part of an afternoon to speak his mission. The two raven-haired women who accompanied him, Clara and Graziella, had kept house for their father ever since a stroke confined their mother to a wheelchair.

Silvio was like a manikin, meticulous and dainty. He pecked at his food like a listless bird and needed to be coaxed into eating at all. His wife, Dina, was huge and fat. She had grown massively heavy in her enforced inactivity. She did not accept her paralysis and railed against it, but she had been obliged to let her unmarried girls take over her chores. Clara had taken to cooking with a passion. She ferreted out recipes from all her many relatives. In her tiny kitchen with its electric cooker and wood-burning stove, she cooked for her large and fussy family. She tried out recipes so complicated that some of them took five days.

We never discovered why Silvio had singled us out as candidates for the secrets of his walnut liqueur. Maybe he had heard that the Scots have an inordinate capacity for holding their liquor, or maybe he'd been surprised to see the Beauties and me breaking an unwritten taboo for women by drinking spirits in a public bar and thought it would be better to have something strong at home to keep us there. Whatever the reason, his stammering friend dictated a shopping list for us to procure by the following day. The recipe for *nocino* was as follows:

> 5 litres of pure alcohol
> ½ kilo of sugar
> 5 lemons
> A handful of cloves
> The finely chopped pulp of 30 green walnuts
>   (before the nut case has hardened)

It was one of Clara's longer recipes: it took forty days.

We bought the goods, and Silvio and the others returned the following evening. The lemons were useless, apparently, because they had not come from a local tree. There was only one lemon left on my tree, and it was a stunted fruit that threatened never to change its steadfast green. The other two baby lemons had been knocked off the tree by stray cricket balls. Having got over her initial shyness, it was the younger, forthright daughter, Clara, who busied herself with the making. Chopping up the rock-hard walnuts with an axe was the most difficult part of the operation. A yellow stain lurked in the outer walnut cases, discolouring hands, nails and clothes.

Once prepared, the ingredients were tipped into a carefully washed and drained glass demijohn, then covered with a secure lid of some sort and stirred night and morning for ten minutes. To fail to stir even for one day, Clara warned us, would cause irreparable damage. Silvio gave us a thick willow stick to stir the mixture with. It looked suspiciously like one of the original missing cricket stumps.

On September 15th, it would be ready for bottling,

Silvio, the high priest of the preparations, told us through his shy, red-cheeked interpreter. Then he vilified the stuck-up character of the Castellani, praised the ultra good-natured Orsolani, and went over everything we had watched and prepared again, with snippets of news and information scattered throughout to keep our attention. They all spoke in the broadest dialect.

'*En dù'èno le ruschiè? Piiele ne una, questa è piena de gniacchera.*' ('Where are the sticks? Get me another, this one's full of mud.')

'*E' la me lè.*' ('It's over there.')

Robbie, whose Italian was creeping along to conversation pitch, understood not a word. They told us of a local Partisan who had been fabled for his love of *nocino* and who had returned to his *cantina* under the eyes of the enemy to raid his own *nocino* and take it back into the hills.

They discussed the known deaths and miracles attributed to *nocino*. They discussed the outcome of the football match they had all watched on the television. During the course of these stammered talks, all our hands turned yellow to the wrist. Only Clara and her sister had hands that were unjaundiced, having come armed with rubber gauntlets.

'Is it true,' the translator asked, staring around him at the four long windows of the kitchen, 'that there are three hundred and sixty-five windows and doors here?'

'No, that was a fabrication.'

'It's hard to imagine, isn't it?' he said in awe, obviously imagining the three hundred and sixty-five windows and doors for all he was worth, already seeing them so clearly in his mind's eye that he would be reporting their existence to the village as soon as he returned.

'And aren't you afraid to be here on your own?' Clara asked me.

I shook my head and was as surprised as she was to

discover that I really wasn't afraid to be there alone. I had been afraid of every house I had ever lived in after dark. Some houses had been worse than others. The castle I had lived in in the Norfolk fens had been like a set from a Hammer horror film. It had not had electricity on its first floor for the first year that I lived there. Although it had been more or less restored, it was severely lacking in sanitation. Despite its size, there was a squalid bathroom fed by rainwater from the lead roof in one wing, and a tiny turret lavatory in the other. I had spent many nights locked into that cramped octagonal turret in guttering candlelight, listening to the knocking of deathwatch beetles in its wooden ceiling and the dragging of peacock's claws like chains across the roof, too terrified to emerge until the arrival of the housekeeper and the morning. It wasn't possible to lock myself into many of the rooms of the villa, given the absence of doors, but I had never felt the need to. After our first fortnight, when the noises of the hills and the empty ruin had settled down into recognizable pattern, I had never felt fear there again.

Clara told me that she was so afraid of the size of the *palazzo* that nothing would get her up there at night, but she would come during the hours of daylight from time to time to inspect the progress of our *nocino*.

Next day, in the village, Regina and Menchina and all our other friends knew as much about our walnut liqueur as we did. The grapevine was fast and efficient, information was ferried up and down the hill, together with advice about this and that day of our *nocino*'s gestation.

In the fields, capsicum peppers swelled out like yellow toads squat to the ground. The high sweet corn made an ever shadier avenue of our road, and its pouches of corn on the cob began to form below the wispy silken beards. These silken strands were gathered by some of the old women and used to make a cooling, not very pleasant drink whose medicinal properties were said to be good for the kidneys.

'Nearly as good as mare's-tail tea, and better than barley water, but not as good as watermelon,' Menchina assured me.

The village abounded in herbal remedies, but most people had switched from natural medicine to monitoring by more conventional doctors and the chemical analysis of their blood at the hospital in Città di Castello. However, the power of certain tisanes like camomile and fennel reigned undisputed, as did the efficiency of mallow for the relief of swollen gums and, first and foremost, of food as the root of good health and a careless diet as the root of all evil.

The year seemed to have expanded in its early months and then contracted from mid-summer on, as though its essence was squeezed there like a concentrated paste: like the paste in the hundreds of bottles of concentrated tomatoes that every family of Orsolani boiled up and stored. These tomatoes were the glut of the vegetable gardens. A great cast-iron pot, an heirloom from harder times, was pulled out in late August or early September and set over a bonfire contained by flat stones. Tomatoes, garlic and basil leaves were then boiled up and bottled. This store of tomatoes, the fruit of every back, front or side garden, then lined the shelves of each *cantina*.

Winter was not worth contemplating without them. The wolves that had until so recently roamed the forests around the village and, metaphorically, threatened every door, would have trembled at the sight. Maria d'Imolo told me that each household made up a minimum of a hundred jars, but usually closer to two or three hundred. She herself made two hundred and thirty that year. This *polpa*, as they called it, was the pride of the cellar. It came after the wine and next to the ham and salamis. Unusually, the *polpa* production was a joint effort: grown by the men but bottled by the women. Such was the power of the tomato, it could break down the sexual barriers. For it was considered to be almost as all-powerful as a Victorian embrocation. If the jars of *polpa* were to have had labels, no doubt they would have said that the contents were not only delicious and nutritious, but also an antidote to snake bite, depression, coughs, colds, fevers and every other ailment known to man. They were the Umbrian equivalent of calves' foot jelly. Whenever one or other of us was ailing, we were invariably given a little jar of *polpa*, to eat with tiny shapes of pasta cooked in a broth made from a freshly strangled hen and *gli odori* (which consisted of celery, parsley, onion and garlic).

The child Iseult still lived almost exclusively on buckets of short pasta served with *polpa di pomodoro*. The sight of so many iron pots full of this elixir ignited her nerves again. Her lists increased and the days of her relentless cleaning returned. With the advent of furniture, her spring-cleaning, if she didn't finish the job, left chaos in her wake. The telephone was her new toy, she spent hours on it. It had even managed to distract her from her facepacks, although sometimes the two were combined. After six or seven hours of scrubbing ornaments in the sink with a toothbrush and soda, she'd call to Paris and recount a fictionalized day to whoever cared to listen. In true Andean style, she described such days as having been spent riding bareback across the hills with her hair streaming out behind her. When I remonstrated with her for her blatant fantasies, she was unrepentant and threw back at me my own frequent lapses from reality.

September 15th arrived, the day of the *nocino*-bottling ceremony. Silvio the Poet arrived in style, dandified and excited and accompanied by four of his five daughters, two sons, and a granddaughter with the looks and allure of a young Gina Lollobrigida. Everyone was dressed in an outfit fit for a ball, with gold and silver lamé predominating. The earlier visits had been slightly strained; Clara and her sister Graziella, I realized, had been positively subdued. This visit was marked by its hilarity. We passed our stirring test, the sieved residue of lemon skins and spices looked as utterly disgusting a sludge as Silvio could have wished, and the decanting began.

All Silvio's children complained about his wild ways. The youngest of his sons was thirty-eight, the eldest sixty. Clara bemoaned having to keep house for her octogenarian/adolescent parent.

'If there's any kind of dancing or merrymaking within walking distance of home, *mi babbo* takes off into the night. A wildness grips him at parties. Sometimes, I'm not exaggerating, he dances on his own in a frenzy, like a madman.' She shook her head. 'I've nothing against dancing, I love it myself, I'm not averse to dancing all night either, but *mi babbo* goes berserk or he pushes his luck. He looks out for the girls with the biggest udders and he buries his head in there. He's had more slaps than a donkey.'

Silvio interrupted. 'At my age, the embarrassment is always worth the result. When you're eighty, you don't care if someone slaps you so long as you get the cuddle and the feel of flesh.'

Clara shook her head again, half-indulgently and half in despair.

'*Mi babbo*, what do you make of him? One of these days . . .'

On the shelf next to my toxic *nocino*, I set the bottles of capsicum peppers in olive oil, of sliced aubergine in chilli oil and garlic, of tiny flat onions in white wine and oil, of *polpa*, the treasured home-grown tomatoes. I even managed to rustle up some basil leaves from the rubble by the end of September to go with them. I had wild strawberries culled from the undergrowth around us and bottled in maraschino. I had blackberries bottled in syrup and made into jam. I had quince preserve and forty two-kilo jars of white peaches in brandy.

My larder was filling and I was so pleased with it that I went around bottling everything in sight. Robbie warned the children to keep moving or I'd bottle them. I turned our kitchen into a witch's cookhouse, full of bundles of drying herbs, both culinary and medicinal. I began to indulge all my own bottled passion for medicinal herbs. Maria d'Imolo approved of all this bottling. It was a pursuit after her own heart. We were stocking up against the winter. It was a shame that we had no chickens or geese, ducks or guinea fowl or pigeons, and not even a pig to fill our freezer and our larder, but we were heading in the right direction with the pickling mania, and she even copied down one or two of the recipes, although the recipe traffic was mostly a one-way system.

Chapter 19

By mid-October, the weather was still blissfully warm. The sudden storms continued, pounding down in tropical torrents. Imolo and the workmen were still pounding away on the top floor, in the Maestro's studio, plastering the three huge spaces, wiring, plumbing and generally consolidating them. The roof joists were weak in several places and fifteen-metre-long chestnut beams were removed and replaced in the underside of the roof. The floors up there were to be of terracotta tiles inlaid with bands of pink and red marble. The stone-cutting machine screeched and whined.

The fallout of their work was a layer of dust that covered everything. I brushed its fine grit from my teeth and out of my hair every day with little effect. It sat over every surface and embedded itself in the pile of any fabric. It got inside cupboard doors and behind glass. It got into our food and sat like a dull skin on the surface of every cup of tea. Imolo said it would take at least a year to get rid of it. He had managed to persuade his wife to come up to the house on a daily basis to help shift it from one room to the next. Maria worked on it with the same zeal as the child Iseult; but Maria was consistent in her efforts. She complained bitterly about her losing battles, but we saw undreamed-of improvements.

Iseult continued to occupy the small room near the top of the stairs, the Arab room, which she had furnished with a high brass bed, a mahogany wardrobe which she kept empty, a chest of drawers and writing table in satinwood and a grey and white Indian rug, upon which all her clothes were heaped.

Allie had a bedroom in what would one day be the nursery flat. His taste was spartan; he liked to keep up a pretence of camping still. He had asked for a bed only and a chair, but Maria insisted on a chest of drawers and a table for his homework. His books and toys were mostly unused, his attentions being turned to the village and the bar, to games of cards, to Medium-sized Daniele and their games of football.

Robbie and I had a suite of rooms: the master bedroom with the french windows-to-be, a dressing room and a large bathroom. For the time being, we used only the bedroom, where our high Italian bed was strategically placed as far away from the four windows as possible to protect it from the rain. It was like a raft. The headboard was painted iron with scenes of the sea and a distant landscape. A loo table occupied the centre of the room, with chairs which we often moved out to our balcony. We kept our favourite books in an octagonal cabinet in one corner, and on my mother's bow-fronted mahogany chest of drawers Robbie had arranged his extensive collection of tiepins, cuff links, collar studs and fobs and my collection of miniature wooden boxes. This chest of drawers was Maria's nightmare. She insisted on dusting it every day but to no avail. In the ceiling, to the left of the loo table, there was a nest of martins which decamped one day in October. At night, when the temperature dropped, the bats swooped in and out of our windows and circled the room, prevented from leaving it to explore the rest of our suite by a crimson velvet curtain.

Five guest rooms alternately stood by or were filled with guests. After the departure of the Brigadier and Miss Myrna for Scotland, there was a lull. Our Dutch friends were due to return with a carload of bulbs, but it was still too early to plant the lilies; too hot, and the land was not yet ready. Despite the daytime temperatures, the evenings had begun to chill and the mornings were misty.

Some shallow market research in the village and among the workforce led us (erroneously) to believe that Sant' Orsola had a temperate climate with mild winters. In my experience, no Italian likes to admit to the coldness of his climate, but I somehow forgot this as we planned our future heating. Guided by Imolo, we had waived any central heating on the first floor. No pipes had been laid under the lovely marble floors. Most of the fireplaces that could have been opened were left closed. The consensus of opinion was that the winters were very short (five weeks or so in duration) and although they could be sharp, it rarely snowed. Regina claimed to remember only one bad winter, in '84. Imolo thought that '87 had been a cold year, but no one spoke of the bitter frosts to come or the regular searing cold of every year.

Menchina, who lived her life in a cycle of migraines, was a perfect windvane. She knew the air currents better than anyone. Wind brought out her red bandanna.

'When the wind comes up from Africa as a sirocco, it's warm and often carries drifts of sand from the Sahara. It's a yellow wind. The east wind is the worst, though. When it beats down from Zeno Poggio, it cracks my head open.'

As though by way of a warning of the blizzards to come, the potted lemon tree developed a scrofulous condition. Its stems and leaves became covered in snow-white flakes, some of which fell like pristine dandruff on to the peat around its roots. On closer inspection, these flakes had legs, lots of them. The lemon tree seemed ready to give up its ghost. Imolo pointed out, not unkindly, but with a hint of infinite wisdom that I found most crushing, that *his* lemon tree did not suffer from such a plague.

'Nor would it. You should have sprayed with copper sulphate in the spring and again during the summer before the lemons formed.'

The one surviving lemon had long since dropped off my tree, together with most of its leaves.

'You should have known that,' Imolo told me. 'Didn't you have lemons in South America?'

We did, but lemons were weeds there, they grew wild, untended and mostly unwanted. It was limes that were used in drinks and fancy bars. Lemons were used for cleaning copper, and for sitting under the shade of their leaves, and nothing else. Once a fortnight, the copper vats in my sugar factory used to be scoured out with lemon juice. It was widely believed, in the Andes, that lemon juice curdled the blood in our veins, so no one in their right mind would eat one. It was useless to try to explain this, it would merely have reflected badly on South America, a place I am wont to defend. Although the Orsolani were so willing to accept outsiders into their midst, they were militantly resistant to accepting any notions that might have damaged the truth of their inherited customs and ideas. For hundreds of years, people had doted on their potted lemon trees here, and not to do so would have been seen as a lack of manners. So I labelled our *nocino* liqueur and kept my counsel.

The storms ceased, the skies stopped turning from blue to a thunderous granite, and no more drops of rain tumbled out of the clouds accompanied by theatrical sound effects. But the last 'summer' storm to occur was more violent than any of the others. The rain fell as balls the size of small lemons. This hail caused havoc with the surrounding tobacco crop. The leaves had begun to be selectively stripped off from the beginning of August, but the main crop stayed in the field, mutilated and left to resprout and strengthen its other leaves. The hailstorm knocked holes in them. It flattened entire hectares of potential crops. The farmers began to sue the government for compensation.

Down at Regina's, the hail and the damage it had caused were the main topics of conversation. Transparent Cenci explained.

'We need the rain, we like it: it saves the reservoirs and all the fatigue of watering. It's only the hail that's bad, otherwise we'd take any amount of storms. Tobacco plants are like drunkards, they need to drink a lot, and they need to keep drinking regularly.' Ceremoniously, Cenci folded his great ungainly hands into his bony lap, and then sighed. 'The land . . . it's so tiring . . . it's so low!'

Meanwhile, the nights had begun to turn so cold that we had to buy extra blankets. The nightly drop in temperature was such that we took to lighting an evening fire in the big kitchen while the wind blew through the corridors and through the gaping stretch of roof over the stairwell, gathering momentum as it funnelled its way up the stairs and round corners, catching extra currents from the open window apertures. The villa had an empty feel to it again.

Even the Irish Beauties had said their tearful goodbyes to Sant' Orsola and left for their village in Galway, despite having been offered several jobs to persuade them to stay. Most of the jobs designed to lure them were of a waitressing nature, but one was truly bizarre. They had been asked to take it in turns to strip down to a tanga and dance in a fishtank at a nightclub somewhere in the hills around Cortona. Neither of them as in the least tempted, but the larger of them was curious.

'I'm six foot tall and there's nothing little about me, how would I be fitting into that tank?'

We were sorry to see them leave and I found that I did

not hold any of their lax habits against them. Regardless of their domestic skills, they'd survived our first summer and provided a great deal of good-humoured support, which would last longer than any amount of washing or washing-up.

The child Iseult, aged sixteen, had decided she wanted to study French in Paris. The film director had offered her the use of his flat while he worked on a script in London, and she liked both him and the idea of using his studio apartment in Pigalle. On every list she wrote, there were always notes to improve her education and to travel. Languages were one of the things she was good at, so she put her name down for the Alliance Française. She told me that during the summer she had hardly managed to tick off a single thing on any of her lists, and at least if she learnt French, she could tick that off. Proposals had been trickling in for her to model in Italy. She had turned them down, but was spurred by them and their promise of fame and fortune to put her name down for a modelling agency in Paris. Then she began to prepare for the packing of her suitcase. It took ten days, after which she left for France, taking the night train from Florence station, weeping out of the window of her couchette. At the last moment, she changed her mind, but the train was already pulling away.

Robbie was preparing for his first solo exhibition, in Rome. He painted frenetically in his makeshift studio, mixing oils and hunting out models from among the work-men. I had reached a state induced only by a room full of chopped onions or the early stage of pregnancy. Once my frantic bottling of fruit and vegetables came to an end, and I stopped dicing any onions, it became clear to everyone what I already knew: a little Duff-Scott was on its way. Robbie was delighted: this would be his first child. Allie was delighted; he told me to make it a boy and asked how many months it would be before he could play football.

Iseult was so pleased she delayed starting school for a few days and returned to Sant' Orsola so that we could have 'girl talks'. Imolo was so thrilled, anyone might have thought he was the father. He took it upon himself to make the announcement to all and sundry, from the man who came to read the electricity meter to a carload of mushroom-seekers on their way to the woods.

Festas were important in Umbria and processions were serious matters, holidays were organized, farming was a part of life, tending a vegetable plot was a duty, raising hens a God-given right, rearing children was a pleasure, but the gathering of *funghi* was a religion. These *funghi* (various kinds of wild mushroom) had a hierarchy, with the squat *porcino* at the top, closely followed by the rarer *boletro* which nestled like a golden egg yolk just underground. Well below these were the *guaitelle* and the *biètte* with their crimson tops. Silvio and Clara's entire family took to the woods from four in the morning until nearly lunchtime, diving into knots of bracken and scrambling in the undergrowth in certain secret parts of the woods searching for *funghi*. Only Dina, Silvio's seventy-year-old paralysed wife, remained behind, wedged into her wheelchair in the care of a grandchild who was studying to be a pianist and filled the village with strains of his music, practising eight hours a day, every day, to complete his exams.

The secret places in the woods were, like every bit of village scandal, whispered and hushed but known to half the world. So he who got there first got the *funghi*; hence the early morning start. On the two occasions when Clara persuaded me to go with them, we left at five, only to find half of Sant' Orsola and a queue of cars with numberplates from as far away as Livorno already in position, combing through the bracken and brambles as though systematically gathering forensic evidence. I carried my basket because I was told that this was what real *funghi* pickers did, but I didn't get much to put in it on my first trip. The two *porcini* that I did find were riddled with tiny maggots and heaved slightly in my basket on their nest of ferns, even when I was standing still. I redeemed myself slightly by gathering several kilos of *biètte*, but since these are a deep red and grow several inches above the ground in clumps, I felt the achievement was fairly minimal.

Robbie, on the other hand, on his first trip out with Clara's brother Licio, gathered twenty-three *porcini* (more than his guide) and thus proved himself once and for all to be a real man. Word travelled fast, and soon congratulations were coming up from the village. I supposed it was like being smiled on by the gods, this ability to find *porcini* mushrooms.

Now that Robbie had been out into the wood, been blessed, and bonded, he was called out to attend other crucial events in the village, like the weekly performance of the local football team. The Irish Beauties had thoroughly recommended the football team, but since their recommendations had been rather generous and generalized, we had disregarded them. It was during the late autumn that Robbie and Allie joined the regular fan club (of three) and began to attend all the games. I used my pregnancy as an excuse to get out of all the functions in the village that required anything more energetic than drinking or dancing. From having been rather shy about taking to the dance floor, I had swung in the opposite direction ever since a young farmer called Domenico, with a congenitally weak intestinal tract and an extremely light step in the polka, had volunteered to give us lessons over the winter.

As we moved through October, Imolo continued his campaign to persuade us to decamp from the upper floors with their tendency to flood and their windows open to the elements.

'It's unhealthy to sleep with fog inside your room,' he used to say several times daily. He tried hard to convince us, but without success. Already the restoration and completion of the first floor, the laying of the entrance hall floor and the connection of all the necessities like light and water and drains had nearly bankrupted us. We were getting on slowly with the top attic floor, but we were waiting for a suitable financial miracle to occur so that we could pay for it. The chances of two such miracles was, we thought, slight. So we were intent on using our rooms despite certain spartan characteristics, of which the intermittent flooding was only one.

After a great deal of haggling, which spun itself out until the onset of winter, we acquired a woodpile which someone had been storing outside our house. He wanted us to buy it because if we did not he would have to shift it, but his asking price was absurdly high. We wanted to buy it because we had no other fuel. The bargaining consisted in our trying to hide the fact that we would actually have paid anything for the woodpile. Left to our own devices, we would have settled months earlier, but we were an associated family, the adopted protégés of Imolo and a couple of other local leaders, so to conduct any local business meant going through them or at least behaving as they would and thus not losing face. Society at Sant' Orsola dictated a great tolerance. Any one of its members could lose their job, their virginity, their wealth, their limbs, their house and even their marbles and still be a respected member of the pack. But to lose face was a tricky concept and one not to be taken lightly. Over major matters, by general consent, the idea of losing face was waived, thus avoiding the vendettas and the ravages of the old south, yet it was a point of pride not to lose face in little things, the token rituals, like how much to pay for a second-hand woodpile.

Just as one can study different influences and trends in the architecture of the various regions of Italy, so too can one study the variations in woodpiles. In northern Umbria, this has been elevated to a popular art form. With meticulous care and a great deal of creativity, each household stacks its wood. Within each stack there are patterns, and the originality lies in the complexity of the pattern, the compactness and exact matching of lengths and breadths. Most of the wood is oak from the self-seeded forests. Most of it is cut by a local contractor and then rolled down through the existing, fifteen-year-old trees to be gathered and hauled away. One tree in three is left, by law. Olive wood is aromatic and burns well. There is still some left from the great frost of 1984. Applewood is rare and smells of cinnamon as it burns. Chestnut wood is good and gives a solid burn, the resinous pines give out a quick high heat, but yew is poisonous and its fumes can be deadly.

'*Eh, bé*!' as Cenci would say, 'this is a world of oak.'

The days continued to be warm enough to eat out in the garden and to sit for hours on the cleared site where there was soon to be an ornate pergola. Its reception committee of six wisterias was already in place, and the plants had just lived through their first drought and survived into what I hoped would be an easier season for all of them. The nightly drop in temperature, though, occurred so suddenly that Robbie, Allie and I were all smitten with colds and a mild kind of flu. Imolo's workforce had also been struck down by this virus. In the village all we heard were tales of woe from stricken flu victims and their relatives.

There was a great fear of illness in Sant' Orsola, combined with an arsenal of practical measures of combat it. The properties of hot and cold foods were known to most local housewives over the age of forty. Thus when the blood was overheated, when there was infection or fever, all fruits (except bananas) had healing properties, as did leaf vegetables, and salad, but not tomatoes (although bottled ones were perfect). Tiny shapes of pasta in *brodo* acted like Italian penicillin. It was like a poultice for all ills, almost a religion. Meat, red meat or game overheated the blood, as did milk, cheese, red wine and potatoes.

At the hint of an ailment, the wisdom of adopting a diet '*in bianco*' was rarely questioned. White, bland foods like a nursery diet plus the inevitable addition of quantities of insipid miniature pasta boiled in an innocuous broth were adopted. Chicken breast, milk, *stracchino* cream cheese and rice were used more readily than drugs. Under every house, racks of tools and bits of machinery were scrupulously cleaned and oiled. The human body too was seen as an endlessly fascinating and complex piece of machinery. Everything was tested and monitored. Progress was commented on and setbacks were discussed. Since the *contadini* had always lived off the land, their work depended on the strength of their bodies. Illness had a simple alphabet that spelt despair. In Sant' Orsola, I found myself dusting off, as it were, past operations, caesarian sections, short comas and drip experiences to use as credentials in those circles where the survival of calamity was seen as an admirable feat. The scars of a surgeon's knife were regarded as medals won in a hard campaign. I had my medals in the scars and memories of many past operations. Survival and subsequent good health could be looked upon as an outwitting of fate, the tricking of the grim reaper. What seemed, at times, like a morbid interest in blood pressure, or the imperfect working of an organ, was also a form of self-defence, a way of combating disease.

Abetting this resistance was the provincial newspaper, *La Cronaca Umbra*, with its mine of information and statistics: 'Second only to the Japanese, the Italians live longer than any other race.' On the other hand, there were always one or two hypochondriacs, who, armed with so much medical information about potential ailments, would reply to a simple greeting such as, 'O, how are you? How are things?' with a mind-bendingly detailed account of the malfunction of a lower intestine, and a nibble by nibble description of their own particular brand of the white diet. The local paper did not say whether newcomers to the country would benefit from that extra decade of life or not, but I noticed that ever since reading about this Italian longevity I had taken to planting slow-growing things in the garden as well as the rampant rocket variety. Thus a wellingtonia and a cedar of Lebanon were down on the garden list to take their places beside the acacia and the eucalyptus trees, and a slow and cosseted clematis had already been allowed in with the wisteria. Although I knew that all the great temperate gardens had been planted by people who realized they would never live to see the full splendour of their designs, I had never been able to accept that my own gardening labours were essentially for another generation. Gardening for me was more a desire to see the fruit of my work than a craving for immortality. I was a selfish gardener: I wanted to design and leave something permanent and lovely, but I also wanted to see it for myself.

It still took a great imaginative leap to look out across the scrubland and hummocked rubble and see this garden. I turned my concentration away from my other thoughts and tried to conjure up this future growth. I imagined myself gathering not only September and October acorns as my neighbours did, but also the fruits of an entire orchard. From the first cherries to the last apples, I conjured up a vision of a pantry stocked with bottled fruits.

The walnut liqueur, the living evidence of something from the garden being put to use, was hibernating on a dresser shelf. The other jars of local produce gave me the vicarious sense of good husbandry. The fifteen-foot-long dresser in the big kitchen had cried out for bottled things, and there they were, a comfort to me in the shortening days.

After it had been decanted, the *nocino* had to be left to stand for a month. My first and only glass of it felled me with such astonishing speed that I was unable to reach my bed from the kitchen, passing out *en route* on the sitting-room sofa. I remained unconscious until the following morning. This short coma was not one I alluded to during medical discussions, nor have I ever dared drink or serve the *nocino* again. Twice, wandering visitors have discovered the stored bottles. My sister Anna was almost knocked senseless by the thimbleful she tried, but a Dutch designer declared it to be 'curiously warming' and drank several glasses of the thick, dark-brown stuff before stumbling away to bed. He was not a happy guest on the following morning, and his pallor was alarming. He insisted on attributing this to his northern blood and a series of late nights. I was told that *nocino* becomes more innocuous with age. Meanwhile, we were waiting.

Chapter 20

October was the month with a general sense of well-being, endowed by the grape harvest, which is called *the* harvest, because it is shared and is the best loved of all the harvests. The small vineyards were picked by rota, with one family helping another. We all pledged to help Imolo and Maria, who had a vineyard cleared from the edge of a wood up on the hill opposite our house.

Our team was made up of Imolo himself, Maria, Imolo's mother and stepfather, Imolo's son Stefano and his daughter Barbara, both in their teens. Their neighbour, Vittorio, who fell off his *motorino* one night and broke his nose but never went to have it reset or stitched, was also there, his broad face permanently stretched into a smile and his lopsided nose distorting what must once have been a handsome face. Vittorio cut his bunches of grapes and philosophized as he did so, comparing his life to the gnarled vines and his feelings to the fruit. Helping with the cutting were two more neighbours, both middle-aged women wearing their traditional housewife's uniform of a cross-over cotton pinafore, which looked strangely incongruous with the big wellington boots on their feet. They told me they were afraid of snakes.

We started at ten, after the sun had risen high enough to dry the dew from the grapes. By one o'clock we were a third of the way through the rows of vines, having filled dozens of buckets apiece. Most of the men carried these buckets back to the wooden crates which would transport them to Imolo's *cantina*. Our hands were stained green to the elbow from the copper sulphate on the vine leaves. At one, we paused to eat bread and salami, pecorino cheese and pears. Everything and everyone was covered in sticky grape juice. Imolo was a happy man, the usual sad expression in his eyes had gone. He had been working as a builder and mason since he was twelve, and at forty-eight he was nearing the time when he could retire. The pension system in Italy was geared to the number of years a man or woman had worked. Contributions to the state for health and pensions were high, but most people could retire in their early fifties. When there was talk of introducing a new system, whereby a man cannot retire until he is sixty-five, the idea was met with outrage. Card games in the bar were stopped to discuss such an outlandish suggestion. 'What's the point of retiring when you're too old to enjoy yourself?' The villagers all worked on into their eighties and nineties, doing heavy manual labour and field work, but it was for themselves. The state could only claim so much of any life, and once the dues were paid, everyone insisted on their freedom.

By six o'clock, the tractor and its trailer were ready to jolt downhill with a cargo of grapes. I felt completely exhausted but I refused to admit it. Allie had cut a high quota and was praised for it. He was so pleased that he asked everyone to assess how many buckets of grapes they had picked so that he could compare his own tally with theirs.

While the men prepared the *mosto* (the pressed grape juice) downstairs in the *cantina*, the women prepared supper. This was a working day, so there were no *crostini*, but there was home-made *tagliatelle* (prepared by Imolo's daughter Barbara) with a *porcini* mushroom and tomato sauce, then there was roast wild pigeon and roast rabbit and a bowl of green salad, followed by pecorino cheese and pears again. The pigeons were served cut into pieces by the same savage secateurs used to clip the bunches of grapes. The delicacy was the charred bald head complete with eyes and beak. As guests, Robbie and I were offered these, but refused, not wishing to deprive Imolo of the pleasure of crunching through the skulls himself. Together with last year's wine, there were bottles of the fresh *mosto*, which was very sweet but delicious.

'*Mosto* bloats,' Vittorio warned us, 'and you'll be up all night if you drink too much of it.'

It was late at night when we made our way home, Allie, Robbie and I, squeezed into our two-seater car. I missed Iseult – never one for any kind of continuous hard work, but somehow always a part of it with her decorative presence. She had been back in Paris for two weeks.

The local shops were like pictorial calendars, stacking up beside them all the accoutrements of whatever activity was taking place in the village at any time. Before the grape harvest, there were plastic tubes, barrels, vats, buckets and stands of secateurs, bottle racks and funnels. By early November, these had changed to the nets and crates needed to bring in the olives. The paucity of gear reflected the low yield of the olive groves, which had yet to recover from the great frost of 1984. The fields around the villa were once slopes of olives; now there was no trace of them as the Sardinian sheep kept for their milk picked over the thistles. Where olives had survived, it was usually as new shoots sprouting from the ancient roots. This was not really an olive area. Further away, towards Assisi, they flourished, as they did in the nearby Tuscan valley of Castiglione Fiorentino, but here they were tiny hard fruits which were caught in swathes of orange netting slung under the trees and then taken away to be pressed.

By mid-November, the winter was beginning to set in. Winds rattled round inside the house, driving so much cold rain into the rooms that some of the bedrooms had become semi-permanent islands of furniture raised on bricks, waiting for more clement weather. Carrying firewood up to the first-floor kitchen became a major task. There were chimney stacks built in all over the house, but only one had been opened up and that was in the big kitchen. It was a giant fireplace and its giant appetite was insatiable. By the end of the month, it was so cold in our windowless bedrooms that we moved down to the first floor, draping more curtains across doorways in an attempt to block out the wind.

We still had our apartment in Venice, although it was now for sale in the hope of settling our debts. We knew we could decamp and go back there until the worst of the cold was over. Imolo, Vittorio and a great many others assured us that the winter was short-lived, so we decided to stay on. I felt decidedly sluggish with my pregnancy, and spent many days watching the fire, staring into its flames and huddling around its embers. Sometimes, when Allie came home from school, we walked in the woods, searching for *funghi* even though we both knew that the season had past.

Work on the villa had slowed to a hibernation rate. Imolo came up every morning with Gigi, his ever-willing mate, and between them they made moulds of the terracotta. They had made a jigsaw of all the pieces unearthed around the property, and these had been reconstructed to provide window surrounds. It was almost all there, but a few bits were missing. There were also chunks of friezework which would need to go round the tower over Robbie's studio when, if, it was ever finished. Each piece of terracotta weighed several hundredweight. With the help of the marble mason, Imolo had tracked down a yellow, rubbery paste from France which was designed for statues. He covered each piece with this paste and then left it to set, peeling it off, boxing it in and then filling it with an orange-pigmented cement. Eventually, he would have all the missing details needed to restore the crumbling façade. But the rubber mould substance didn't like the cold, and it reacted strangely. Imolo and Gigi, up to their armpits in lurid yellow paste, found it hugely amusing and kept calling me down to watch.

November was the hardest month. Getting used to the cold was a shock to our systems. Our car didn't like it either, and often as not it refused to start. A local mechanic came up and tortured its engine from time to time, forcing it back into action, but it seemed to suffer irreversible damage during these sessions. It started, took us down the hill (and sometimes back again), but it had begun to develop a consumptive cough and intermittent groaning. No matter what other cars a family owned, everyone had a Fiat 500, a tiny kind of bubble car which could cope indefatigably with the bumpy dirt roads, the improbable gradients and the vagaries of the climate. Imolo offered to find us one.

When Robbie's father died, he left him the 1924 Rolls-Royce that he had personally reconstructed over a period of twenty years. It was dauntingly perfect and the size of a small coach, a navy-blue convertible worth a small fortune and needing as much care and attention as a newborn child. It needed an air-conditioned garage in the summer and heated accommodation over the winter so that its ash panels would not warp. It needed a smooth road and an occasional easy ride. Neither of us thought it could cope with the spartan conditions we were living in, even if we had brought it indoors. At first this had seemed like a possibility, since the downstairs hall had contained the wrecked contents of a farm garage when we first saw the villa. The winter was too cold, and the cement dust problem too severe, even to contemplate this any more. So our dreams of cruising around Sant' Orsola in its soft leather seats were stored away with other impractical ideas, like a bear house and an underground Arabic pool, and our entry into the *Mille Miglie* race for vintage cars lapsed.

Meanwhile, Imolo came up with a different navy-blue convertible, a Fiat 500 selling for the princely sum of £400. This became our family car. We had found that we could (quite illegally) get our family of four into Robbie's spluttering sports car by careful squeezing and lying on top of each other, but now with a new child on the way it was no longer possible. The Fiat 500 proved to be such a good, popular and lasting car that the factory had had to stop making it: it never gave up and people just weren't buying as many new cars. Imolo had read somewhere that the patent was going to be sold to China, where I hoped it would fare as well as it had in Italy.

Iseult, home early from Paris for Christmas, drove the new car round and round the garden while Allie cowered by the beds of dormant lilies imploring her to stop. Iseult was on a high and even speedier than usual; she kept the ghetto blaster blaring at an open window, bribing her younger brother to go upstairs to change the cassette while she sang along, racing the car around like a Dodgem at the funfair. She had all but abandoned her string of local admirers in favour of Michael, the film director, with whom she was having an affair – confident that this time it was different. By different, I took her to mean that it might be longer than the statutory three weeks before her attention drifted to someone else. She was keen for him to come out for Christmas.

Maria d'Imolo had started working part-time at the villa. She came up every morning to get Allie off to school and then helped me. She moved from one area of the house to another, swathed in shawls, scarves and gloves. Everyone in Sant' Orsola had central heating and she was stunned by how cold it was in our house. She told me about her sisters and her brother in Nice and about the rigours of her childhood there. She protected our interests jealously and doted on Allie, whom she often took home with her to the comfort of her kitchen.

Every day, the frosts became more severe and the sun did not thaw them until nearly lunchtime. Often, in the afternoons, it was still warm enough to sit out, but the nights were cruel. Outside the microclimate of our house, everyone seemed studiously to ignore the encroaching winter. The bars were too cold for us to linger, but the men still sat around playing *briscola*. We seemed to be getting strange looks from some of the villagers, and for the first time there was an uneasiness in their approach. Estelio, the headman of the *proloco*, came up to the house several times as though he wanted to say something, but departed again after a drink and some pleasantries. Maria told me what I already knew, that Estelio had something on his mind, but she feigned ignorance as to what it was.

It was Paul who eventually told us what the trouble was. It seemed that the derelict Villa Orsola had been the site of the annual New Year dance for as long as anyone could remember. It was the only indoor space big enough to dance in. In previous years, the abandoned vehicles had all been hauled out, and four hundred Orsolani had celebrated the New Year together. Now that we had bought the place, they had nowhere to go. So could they come and dance in our hall? I had been fearing some terrible social blunder and and wondering if the honeymoon period of our stay in the parish was about to come to an abrupt end. We all liked the thought of this dance (we had even learnt to polka), so we told them, via Paul, that the space was theirs for the night of *Capo d'anno*.

By the time we went down for our shopping the next morning, everyone seemed to know this, and the air was cleared. I was thumped on the back and squeezed on the elbow so many times during the morning that I felt quite mauled by the time I took my increasingly ungainly figure back up the hill.

Iseult, realizing as though for the first time that Christmas was still over three weeks away, returned to Paris, catching the night train from Florence again, laden with suitcases full of her (and my) best clothes.

Chapter 21

For some time now, our country walks had been interrupted by bursts of gunfire, as huntsmen endeavoured to wipe out the local bird population, taking pot shots at anything with wings bigger than a butterfly. This had always struck me as a gruesome exercise, mitigated only by the relish with which the poor little victims were later eaten. The local men defended their right to hunt so keenly that they claimed there would be a revolution if this basic right were taken from them. Imolo was one of the few men in the village who didn't take part in these excursionary massacres. As the guns popped over the hills, bringing down wild pigeons, blackbirds and larks, he shook his head sadly and said it was a pity to take the life of anything so free. In this, we of the *palazzo* agreed, but all attempts to make this point to the huntsmen were in vain. They argued that this was something that their ancestors had been doing for centuries and it was their God-given right, in a country riddled with bureaucracy and regulations, to gain the freedom of the woods every year and complement their diet with the birds of the air. After the birds, it would be the turn of the wild boar, and then anything else that roamed the wood on four legs.

Given this penchant for slaughtering any animal other than cats, dogs and horses, the motley assortment of animals

that accompanied the travelling fair which stopped at Sant'
Orsola were lucky to leave the village alive. For a week,
the patch of waste ground beside the bar that usually
served as a football pitch for Allie and his friends was taken
up by swirling swings, coconut shies and a collection of
rather miserable-looking llamas, a balding monkey, a parrot
and a neurasthenic mule. On two sides, long luxurious
silver caravans housed the showman and his ten children.
In the evenings, he would stroll across to the bar in his
high-heeled boots and red bandanna and plant himself
between the card tables and the counter, blocking that
narrow space with his large frame. From this point at
centre stage he would regale all who cared to know (and
anyone else in earshot, regardless of their willingness to
listen) with an account of his life and trials as a fairground
man and a father.

The word on the street was that one of the showman's
daughters had fallen in love with a local lad and the affair
was looking serious. Rumours often took as long as a day
to reach us up at the villa, that being the interval of time
between one visit and another from Maria d'Imolo. In the
village proper, gossip spread like spilt wine, seeping into
every thread of every household. After a week, the funfair
was dismantled and towed away, but the rumour of ro-
mance persisted. There was not only talk of an engagement,
there was talk of a marriage. Engagements in Sant' Orsola
seemed to last from five to ten years, so no one got unduly
excited by the thought of a *fidanzamento*. A wedding, on
the other hand, meant a big party, to which, at some point
during its day's duration, everyone in the village would be
invited to join in the feast.

The festival calendar was steering inexorably towards
Christmas (*Natale*) and, for Italy, the far more celebrated
festival of the New Year (*Capo d'anno*). Christmas was still
a religious festival here, and little else. Most families draped

some token decoration over a conifer in their garden, or, often as not, a magnolia grandiflora with its wide evergreen leaves, but the main decoration was the *Presepe*, or nativity scene, reconstructed in a corner of every house, usually occupying anything up to a quarter of the sitting room. The shops filled with traditional Easter fare, stuffed pigs' feet and lentils, nuts, dried figs stuffed with almonds and stacks of boxed *panettone*. The *panettone*, together with bottles of sweet, sparkling white wine, were a must in every household. They were widely exchanged as presents, so, by the end of the season, one's *panettone* collection could look like a small pyramid. Each box contained a high sponge bread in a jelly-mould shape, which was then doused in icing sugar and eaten in giant weightless wedges.

There were private slaughter sessions in preparation for both Christmas and the New Year. Geese got their necks wrung and ducks bit the dust. Capons were more popular than turkeys, and at least one mature hen, thinking to have escaped the earlier cullings and looking forward to a relatively easy life of laying eggs and gorging grain, found itself the main ingredient in the vat of broth which was the mainstay of Christmas dinner in every family. After long hours of preparation, the *cappelletti* pasta squares were cooked for two minutes in a pot of rich chicken broth. This was a meal that could be prepared some hours beforehand, thus freeing an entire family, including the cooks, to attend mass.

Christmas Eve was also observed religiously, only fish being eaten all day, and midnight mass with the full village choir (which was almost as large as the village, it seemed) was full of people chatting in the back rows and huddles of men lingering outside the church smoking.

The real feast, though, the feast from which no one was expected to get up for at least six hours, the feast after which all normal digestive systems were meant to feel deeply affected for several weeks was the dinner of *Capo d'anno*. We had been told by Estelio and Imolo that we were not to do anything towards preparing our own version of this meal. Dinner would be served communally at the *campo sportivo*. Maria dropped many gentle hints about dress standards. Clearly to the Orsolani it was the equivalent of black tie, which meant Sunday best, which in Sant' Orsola meant, particularly for women and nubile girls, an astonishing array of outfits. These outfits were really more like costumes than clothes. They made few concessions to what would normally be considered good taste, in fact they were gratuitously gaudy, provocatively skimpy and trimmed with a mixture of gilt, fake jewels and fake fur, with much ingenuity being put into cramming as many of these trimmings on as a piece of cloth could hold. Maria had become the protector of our image, and I could see she was worried about how we would turn out for such a major occasion, given that I in my ungainly new shape was unable to squeeze myself and the coming baby into any of my dresses.

On the evening of December 30th, a convoy of trucks and Fiat 500s surrounded the villa. The vehicles in the convoy communicated by means of the traditional volleys of shouts and repeated use of the horn. Car horn language is important in Italy, rarely conforming to international traffic connotations. Convoy car horns blasting in unison signify that wedding guests after the service are off to have a good time, and the sub-language of horns all stems from this. So, if three cars making their way along a road or up a hill begin to beep the beeps are saying, aren't we having a good time, isn't this fun? When the numbers are tripled, inevitably, it's another party.

Further rounds of shouting filled the otherwise still night air, ballooning breath in the frost as we watched from the kitchen window. Stacks of planks, trestles, grape crates and sundry other things were being unpacked from the trucks, to a continuous stream of '*Dio buonos*' as the tipsy crew struggled with their loads. After the banging, swearing and shrieks of laughter had died down, there was a lot of sheepish calling from outside the house, followed by Imolo arriving and announcing that everyone was too embarrassed to come in.

'It's such an inconvenience for you,' he explained, 'and we'd just like you to know that you can still change your minds. Say the word and we'll load the stuff back on and clear off.'

This had all been gone over innumerable times during the past two weeks. Our assurances had been given in every form other than a sworn affidavit that we were really pleased to be hosting the dance. We knew too that, by now, some four hundred people had been invited from all over the hills and that on the eve of the event, no one had the slightest intention of cancelling anything; yet the coy charade continued for some time, with Robbie relaying bottles of wine down to the crew while delegates from amongst them shouted up apologies through the kitchen window.

Eventually, the musicians arrived to set up their sound system and the pretences stopped instantaneously. Then the team sub-divided and with extraordinary dexterity set up the trappings of the party. Once they had finished and their temporary territorial rites had been staked out, they all became very businesslike and confident. Some more of them would be round on the following morning to place the fireworks on the hillock in front of the villa. Then a last glass of wine was thrown back, and there was a brief debate as to whether I had got the dates wrong about my pregnancy because I looked far more advanced than I was admitting to. The five men of the *proloco* who had been up to deliver token Christmas presents to the children (arriving on a tractor with sleigh bells and a very drunken, very large Father Christmas, who staggered up the stars apologizing for his state – we were the last house on his round and the endless toasts had crossed his eyes) warmed themselves at the fire; the others, some ten in all, hung back and shouted from their huddle in the doorway.

Our dyspeptic dancing master, Domenico, was still a bit worried about our performance and he had arranged to come up just before midnight for a last-minute practice of our waltzes and tangos. We were to go on show, trying out our rather tentative routines, and he was worried about our *contragiri* or counterturns. Would we make him lose face? It was well known that he had been coming up to teach us in the big kitchen every morning. Maria would clear away the glasses and empty wine bottles and move back the kitchen table and chairs, laughing to herself. For, as in Latin America, it is incomprehensible to a native that anyone upon hearing the music would not know the steps – a two-year-old would know them – so lessons seemed a bizarre notion.

'Don't you mind?' Maria asked. 'Everyone's laughing at you.' I tried to explain that being laughed at was better than either having my insteps crushed or tripping up unwitting partners. Nothing, though, it seemed, was worse than being laughed at: losing face. This *brutta figura* ruled life, the fear of ridicule was boss. Which was why Domenico laboured on with our counterturns until two in the morning, anxious that we should do well. By the time I got to bed I was quite confident about all four of the traditional dances, but Robbie and I were both half-crippled by the muscles aching down the backs of our calves.

After the meal at the *campo sportivo* and so many shared bottles of sparkling wine that the flying corks made the refectory sound like a battlefield, we made our way through the biting cold to the *palazzo*. Despite several gas cylinder heaters, the downstairs hall had the temperature of a meat safe. Pietro the last Castellano was the doorman, supposedly checking tickets to exclude any gatecrashers, but actually weaving around without moving his feet, swaying and grinning in all directions, barely keeping his balance as people pushed past him to escape the cold night air. There were two accordionists and the same porphyry-faced, near-apoplectic violinist. Literally hundreds of people we had never seen before clung to the dank walls, while some forty couples warmed up and displayed their ball-room gear, gliding between the pillars.

The last four months of the restoration job, before the workforce dwindled to its winter core, was dedicated to the laying of a pink travertine marble floor and the meticulous repointing of the stone-arched pillars. At the time, this had seemed an unnecessary excursion from the central purpose of fixing up the main part of the house, but now we could see that it was crucial. Imolo must have guessed all along that the dance would continue to be held in this hall, and now everyone was marvelling at his alchemy. There was a constant stream of traffic up and down the main stairs as Imolo led guided tours of locals around the bits he had done. Imolo never danced. He was about the only man who didn't. Even Allie's schoolfriends took their turns stepping conscientiously through the tangos with their mothers and sisters. There were young girls in skin-tight leotards, and young girls in sequined mini-skirts, there were old women with suede booties and moustaches, there were immensely fat middle-aged matrons and tiny, bird-like women all embracing their partners.

The men ranged from seven-year-olds in bow-ties and jackets to spotty adolescents to handsome blades and their less fortunate peers, stocky older men and doddering ancient men, all stepping out in their varying degrees of drunkenness. Everyone we had ever seen in the village was partying. The workmen were all there with their wives and families. Silvio was reaching up into the fullest breasts. Exploding Head (who looked as though half a pound of gelignite had just gone off somewhere behind his nose) was teetering around the room, Snake Head was there with all his brothers, their tiny heads emerging from huge starched collars. Menchina from the bar had come, as had the postman and the marble man, the butcher and his stunning young wife (the one who looked like a version of Gina Lollobrigida and is the pin-up of half the valley).

The wine flowed, as did the fizzy orange without which no party seemed to be complete, but this was a dance, a serious dance, and the crowd danced on until five o'clock in the morning, interrupted only by the arrival of the New Year, when the fireworks went off and there was an intermission while four hundred people all kissed each other twice. After this, there was more sparkling wine and baskets of *panettone* cake and *porchetta* sandwiches. In what was once the Irish Beauties' kitchen, an entire pig with its head intact was being sliced up from the tail inwards. *Porchetta* were always roasted whole, having been stuffed with long fennel stalks and garlic.

After the break, the dancing swirled on. It was so cold that we had to dance to keep warm. Robbie and I committed no major blunders and managed to glide among the pillars with several partners. Domenico was a happy man. Every few dances he escorted me on to the floor so that we could do a really complicated counterturn routine just to show off. After 2 a.m. I was completely exhausted and took myself and my unborn child off to bed, sneaking away to do so. The music pounded up the stairwell and the accordionists seemed to be playing inside my head. Iseult and her new fiancé, Michael, danced tirelessly. Michael learnt to dance at school, and Iseult was taught by the police chief of Casole d'Elsa, who was once a professional dancer. Robbie stayed up till the end, draining the barrels of wine with Pietro, who remained, miraculously, on his feet all evening swaying in the blasts of cold air by the door, the postman, Estelio, Imolo and a knot of dancers.

Next day the entire house smelled like a giant ashtray, and the hall floor was ankle-deep in plastic cups. Immediately after lunch, the same crew of the *proloco* who set up the party were all be-aproned and swabbing down the wine-mottled floor like a platoon of garrulous dailies. By dusk, the hall and the alleyway were immaculate, and far cleaner than they had ever been before.

Upstairs, at the end of the long corridor on the second floor, two of our original kittens and their mother had all given birth to litters of kittens, thus bringing our resident feline population up to twenty. Maria henceforth combined her tasks as housekeeper with a guerrilla war to keep these apparently untameable wild cats and their offspring out of the house. Her plans were continually sabotaged by Iseult and Allie, who found their unhousetrained habits less distressing than Maria. Without doors, it was a losing battle. I credit the eventual arrival of doors in our second spring entirely to Maria's tenacity: she plagued both Imolo and the carpenter until they appeared.

Chapter 22

Having nominally hosted the dance, we became heroes overnight. It seemed that from that moment, we could do no wrong. Even the teams of huntsmen, thirty-six strong, camping by the shrine of the Madonna in shifts to lay claim to their wild boar patch would greet us with cheers as though we were members of their families. We found ourselves inundated with offers of pieces of wild boar and more shares of pigs to be slaughtered than we could contemplate. Eventually, Imolo chose us half a pig and oversaw its conversion into bacon, salami, sausages and raw ham. The pigs were killed during the first days of January. All over the village, vats of water were boiled over bonfires and bags of salt stood by to treat the bacons, while Tonino the pig butcher made his way from house to house with his knives and his hacksaw. My 'interesting condition' excused me from having to witness this grue-some ritual, but Robbie, alas, had no such excuse and was called down to consult and praise several times during the drinking-cum-slaughtering session that took place in the Irish Beauties' kitchen.

Between the pigs and the carnival at the beginning of March, there was nothing but bitter cold. Life was a relay race of wood and more wood. People began to drift up from the village to experience first-hand the growing legend of our cold house: outside there were inches of frost over my lily beds with hoar frost and icicles hanging from the trees. Inside, there was ice in our newly installed bath. Our Italian electric blanket, a present from Maria and Imolo with a contribution from Silvio's daughter Clara, who sometimes came up to help and had already been asked to give me a hand with the new baby when the time came, made bed not only bearable but bliss for a full three weeks. Being a local blanket and abiding by the same rules as local food – no additives and nothing from beyond the confines of the neighbourhood – it had no unsightly additions like a thermostat or any kind of control. You just plugged it in or pulled it out. When it set fire to our bed, narrowly missing us and filling our room with highly toxic fumes, we were only saved from suffocation by the myriad draughts from the plastic sheeting over our four bedroom windows and by the two draughty curtains that posed as doors. After the fire, the like of which several blanket users in the village had also experienced, our bed reverted to a mattress so chilled that for the first twenty minutes it gave the impression of being a mortuary table, with three tiny islands of heat generated by quick-freeze hot-water bottles.

In February, long after spring had been promised, it snowed. Overnight, a blizzard drifted over Sant' Orsola and transformed its surrounding hills into an arctic landscape, cutting us off and providing the *proloco* with another perfect excuse for gathering, drinking and traipsing round in groups of Michelin men to check out each and every family, tanking up in their *cantinas* and then moving on. Our friend Paul, in his isolated cottage in the woods far beyond the village proper, was advised to abandon his home and walk out towards them as they cleared the hill track with a tractor. For the next few weeks, he stayed with us, snowed in, but within trudging distance of the shop and services. Despite its difficulties, everyone loved the snow. At three o'clock each afternoon, the villagers, unable to get to work, convened outside the church for a snow fight. Even Don Annibale the priest's ninety-year-old mother joined in when she picked her way out to her woodpile. There was sledging on the steep hill between the church and the bar, turning the village into a noisy playground. Iseult, home from Paris with a bad kidney, and Allie built up piles of frozen munitions worthy of the Venetian Arsenale and pelted visitors to the villa. By comparison, the carnival seemed rather tame, redeeming itself only by a second dance held in our hall. This time it was a fancy-dress affair which seemed to be attended entirely by women, until as the night wore on, the men in drag began to grow stubble.

When the snow melted, there were some minor floods in the valley, most notably in Silvio's new workshop. His boxes and tins of cobbler's nails and tacks and his stone sculpting tools all needed drying out. On the morning of the flood, Silvio sat on a large stone behind his house with his head in his hands and sobbed, shaking like a frail bird with a broken wing. Not only had his tools been damaged, but a lifetime's hoard of porno magazines had all been soaked and the glossy pages had stuck together. It was days before he lost his bedraggled look of ashen shock and returned to his usual rounds.

Having despaired of the climate and resigned ourselves to a life of chilblains, the first days of March heralded the return of the sun. Or rather, the return of its heat, because the sun had never been absent. All through the winter, there was a brightness about the light, and the days were cold but sparkling. March days were warm enough not only to sit out in the afternoons, but also to eat out in the garden, where there were slow but sure signs of a crop of lilies coming up. These proved to be a temptation too great for our neighbour's pigs, which came marauding in herds of anything up to thirty and systematically followed my lines of planting. Maria temporarily abandoned her campaign against the cats to join me in my war on these new invaders. The garden began to be divided into little fenced compounds.

Easter was approaching and I felt almost as excited about it as the ladies I met in the village shop. Our first batch of visitors this year were coming to stay. Now that parts of the house were furnished, I hardly noticed the almost total absence of any plaster on the upper walls. The tattered Indian carpets were big enough to cover most of the ungainly concrete floors. There were certain angles in certain rooms where, squinting, I could hardly notice their unfinished state.

The big thing at Easter, it seemed, was to make and then eat a local sweet bread called a *cerumia*. The importance of this *cerumia* is not so much its taste as the toil involved in producing it. The most important part of the recipe was an early start – 4 a.m. at the latest – and the ritual heating of an old bread oven. Then the dough was kneaded for many hours.

The *cerumia* was made by teams of women, not one of them having sufficient stamina to complete the task single-handed. In turns, the enormous vat of dough was mauled and manhandled until it was deemed ready. The making of the *cerumia* was a local female equivalent of carrying the cross. It produced, towards dusk, a gathering of utterly exhausted women and a batch of up to two dozen golden cakes. All over the village, the smell of baked bread wafted from *cantinas* and back gardens. Clara's neighbours had replaced the traditional bread oven with a wood-burning stove that chugged its smoke into their cherry trees like a toy engine stranded on grass.

The first disappointment of the *cerumia* ceremony was in

the tasting. It was a singularly insipid cake, or a disturbingly sweet loaf of bread. It didn't earn its rank in either category. The second disappointment was that once it had been crowned with a ritual scattering of multicoloured hundreds and thousands, it started to go stale at an alarming speed. We became the recipients of several *cerumias*, which we were obliged to taste and judge on their various merits. Try as I might, I could discern no difference in any but the burnt. All of our visitors were either bloated by their own family batches or were unaccustomed to the blandly stale gigantic slices of this high bread: I hadn't the heart to throw my *cerumias* away, so they sat, growing daily harder in the bread bin. They had a remarkable resistance to mould. Seven weeks later, they were still haunting the kitchen.

After the real work of the *cerumias* had been completed, a last-minute batch of cakes was baked. These were the basic *crostini*, a lattice of sweet short pastry covered in quince jam, the *torcola* with its dozen fresh eggs, and a low custard tart. There was no finesse in Umbrian baking, but the local cakes were delicious in their heavy way, and were it not for the obligatory wedge of *cerumia* accompanying each of them, matching them slice for slice, I could circle the village endlessly, glutting myself on them with their complementary sips of lethally strong coffee.

The run up to Easter entailed the blessing of eggs in every household. The eggs, we were told, must be our own, but we were still the only family not to keep chickens. Buying a carton of eggs at the local shop seemed like cheating. As I bought them, several worried shoppers asked if they were to be blessed. I had already been warned that this would be a shame. I pretended that the eggs were for baking, which was an even more unthinkable contingency. A chorus of concerned old ladies assured me that no cake would ever work if I tried to make it with shop-bought eggs.

'They have to be fresh,' they told me and smiled protectively, amused that I should even think of attempting such a silly thing. Our usual supply of eggs from Regina's bar had dried up – the hens had all been eaten by a fox.

I spent the afternoon constructing a hen house out of the abundance of debris under the villa. Once it was completed, I enlisted Maria to drive me to a hen shop. We drove for some fifteen minutes and then stopped beside a petrol station at a small, stranded ironmonger's. The owner led us through the shop to a wire hen-highrise at the back. Then followed a long discussion, from which I gleaned that white chickens grew faster and were easier to pluck, but they got splayed feet if left as layers. Speckled hens were the biggest, but not the best, while small red hens gave the most regular eggs. I purchased three small red hens, which were unceremoniously yanked out of their fourth-floor coop and their feet tied up with string. A large plastic shopping bag was then torn at one corner and the hens were thrust, protesting, into it head first, whereupon they became entirely mute and rode home in the back of Maria's Fiat 500 protesting only silently by ejecting liquid *guano* over my legs.

'You'll have eggs tomorrow morning,' the ironmonger guaranteed.

There were six days to Easter. We needed one egg for each of the family and one for each of our three awaited guests to get through the blessing ceremony. Twenty-four hours before Easter Sunday the hens had finished their corn, grouted their shack with excrement, but there were no eggs. When Don Annibale, the priest, came round with his acolyte, he blessed nine shop-bought eggs. Before doing so he asked me kindly.

'Do you keep hens, signora?' and I could honestly answer, 'Yes.'

Chapter 23

The start of April was like the start of a race. The lilies were shooting up, the martins were back, nesting in the eaves and in every available corner of the still unpainted ceilings. The workmen were back. The workforce was up to twelve, but it felt far more than that crawling all over the house, building as frantically as the martins and swallows to get our nest ready for the birth of our baby. Iseult was also back, and determined not only to get married from week to week, but also to have a massive party. And lastly, financing some of the above, our flat in Venice had been sold and preparations were underway to move its furniture through the narrow canal in front of it to the mainland and down to Umbria, to fill some of the spaces that Imolo and his team were suddenly getting to the point of reclaiming as rooms.

With great difficulty, I persuaded Michael and Iseult to postpone their wedding from the May date they wanted to the end of June, which was the earliest I could reasonably manage since I knew I had to go in for a caesarian section. After a lot of bartering and haggling, the date was fixed for exactly three weeks after the birth, and our life was filled with lists. There were guest lists, wine lists, food lists, sleeping lists, musical lists, transport lists and many more. Michael and Iseult both had many friends and she had inherited and enhanced my delusions of grandeur. She wanted a party that would last for three days. She also wanted a hundred guests from abroad, plus the entire village to attend. The telephone rang incessantly with helpful and unhelpful suggestions from guests. What sounded like the least helpful suggestion actually developed into a sore temptation at certain points before the proceedings. David Kirke, the founder of the Dangerous Sports Club who was at Oxford with Michael, called to confirm that he would be coming. He had gathered that we now had a crane on the site while work went on to restore the tower, and suggested that we attach a bungie rope (his invention many years before) to the top of the crane and drop the guests off, for fun. He admitted that it would take about seventeen guests (and casualties) to ascertain the correct length of this bungie rope. Daniele, an opera singer whom we had met on our travels and been close to for years, called to say that he would bring from Florence all the musicians and singers we might need, free of charge. Another friend, from Norfolk, volunteered to organize a cricket match for the last day of the party.

Maria looked on in despair while the cement dust churned up all over the house and pneumatic drills pierced through the stonework. There was now a mesh of scaffolding along two sides of the villa. I had always catered for parties myself in the past, but Maria prevailed upon me not even to try this time, for the sake of the baby. Between us we hired a chef from Città di Castello, who more than tripled our existing shopping lists, thus making the five hundred guests seem nearer five thousand. Trucks and lorries queued to get into the drive. They were delivering slabs of marble, basins, sand, cement, wine, soft drinks, groceries and presents.

I had never seen so many wedding presents. The Orsolani didn't believe in tokens, they clubbed together in groups of three or four families to buy embarrassingly extravagant presents. Lorries came up at the rate of three or four a day, carrying a washing machine, a fridge, a television, pots, pans, rugs, dinner services, furniture, Bavarian glasses, tea services, marble statues, majolica columns, ornate stoves and so on, until an entire large room was heaped with presents from the villagers, many of whom we had only met once or twice, if at all.

By way of gratitude, the party escalated. We felt we must have more entertainments, fireworks, another dance, a picnic packed with every delicacy. To begin with, our menu was half French and half Italian. Maria was not happy about this. Very gently, but with consummate skill, she persuaded us to give an entirely Umbrian feast, ranging more widely than the limited confines of Sant' Orsola but still Umbrian. As soon as this was agreed, the *proloco* volunteered to help. They put forward twenty-five men and women to fill all the posts, from making the *crostini* and the sauces for the pasta, to grilling the meat on open-air barbecues, serving, dish-washing, minding the parking and providing the tables and chairs and linen cloths needed to seat so many diners. When it became clear that we could not seat everyone and still get around the tables to serve, Maria suggested we sit the hundred and forty foreign guests down for lunch and then have five buffets for the other meals.

At this juncture, I had never been to an Italian wedding, although I had seen and heard many processions of hooting cars winding their way through the village. I thought we were giving the party of the century, a 'do' so memorable that it would go down in village history. Despite all the big parties I had given in other times and other places, I had never embarked on catering on this scale or in such lavish abundance. The entertainments were almost an after-thought, a way of getting from meal to meal. What I didn't know was that in Sant' Orsola and its outlying villages, at least, a wedding was something that people saved up for over twenty years or more. Local weddings didn't last for three days, but they did consist of three massive meals, literally thousands of pounds' worth of flowers, unlimited drink and a lot of dancing. So we were doing what any local parents would have done in our place. We just had more organizing to do, since our guests were coming from all over the world. In order to keep abreast of the organization, we kept making lists.

Everything was in turmoil, not least because it looked as if there was no chance of finishing the second-floor bedrooms and the tower before the wedding. Outside, Policarpo and his brother Giovanni, both with incredibly small heads and no necks, trailed around in the wake of a bulldozer trying to coax up six geometric sections of lawn before the wedding day. Battling with the heat and the fallout of cement dust, they were out at all hours, sprinkling and sowing what stubbornly continued to look like expanses of mud.

Nothing seemed set to go easily with the party, so when I went into hospital to have my caesarian section, carrying my suitcase of baby clothes and a bundle of wedding lists, I felt only the outcome of the operation could be relied on with any certainty. I was admitted to the maternity ward on my appointed day and lumbered up the dipped marble stairs in a truly elephantine state. Florence Duff-Scott emerged as one of the smallest babies I have ever seen outside of an incubator. She was the first native Umbrian in our family.

The day after she was born, a nurse came up from the floor below and said that Iseult was just underneath me in Women's Medical, where she had been admitted with kidney stones, struck down in the wee hours on her way to a discothèque.

'Tap on the floor,' the nurse said, 'and she'll hear you, she's a bit down about missing the wedding.'

Two days later, a distraught big daughter limped into my room to keep me and my little daughter company and the lists continued. Day by day, dozens of visitors squeezed through the undergrowth of bouquets of pink flowers sent, like Iseult's wedding presents, by people I didn't really know. Every day Maria travelled in to see me, bringing news, food and lists. It was stiflingly hot in the hospital and the combination of the heat and the mounting problems arising over the party were driving me mad. Bakers, grocers, the chef, the taxi-drivers, the wine merchants, fishmongers and florists all had queries and they all brought them to my bedside. I have often wondered whether Florence learnt to speak so early and with such utter fluency in the local dialect as a result of having been bombarded from birth with those hundreds of wedding questions.

When Florence was twelve days old I took her home, back through fields of gangly tobacco and budding sunflowers, past the green-brown earth pigment of raw umber and the reddish tinge of burnt umber which were all around. I felt a huge sense of relief on entering the village and going past the familiar landmarks of olive press and big house, the island of old stone cottages huddling up a lane to the church and the school at the top, the main street winding past the bar with its rampant Virginia creeper, the shop, the petrol pump, then the new street with the butcher, florist and a handful of houses, each with a wide unfinished façade staring out in dull cement over flourishing allotments. For the first time, I saw these new buildings not as spoiling the look of the village so much as helping to keep it together. I held Florence's tiny swaddled body closer to me as the car bumped past the Confraternity's church with its frescos of flagellation and crucifixion, then we turned on to the dust road that led uphill to the *palazzo*. On the corner, at the bar, nothing had changed. Regina was berating her drunken husband as she stood braced backwards with a cigarette in one hand and a dead rabbit in the other, swinging the furry corpse round in a menacing way, shouting, while her customers got on with their tumblers of cloudy white wine and aimed their *bocce* balls down the lumpy sand of the court.

On a bend in the dust road, the taxi almost collided with the *apé* (a three-wheeled motorbike with two seats and a tiny trailer, for which no driving licence was required) of Gianni and frail old Cenci, Gianni with his voice appliance grinning at the wheel, Cenci with his unnaturally big ears lolling around beside him. Then the road bent again past Cenci and Nunzia's rambling old rented farmhouse which overflowed into Maria del Gallo's more compact smallholding which she shared with Beppe, her ancient, incoherent husband who communicated almost exclusively in sheepish smiles and exclamations. Beyond her house there was a walnut tree and a crest of rock, and above that sat our villa. After so many years of perpetual motion, of living on trains and out of trunks and in hotels and out of suitcases, and in rented accommodation which rarely lasted longer than a few months, I was returning home to a house I had now lived in for over a year, with a new child who would have the opportunity of growing up in a village full of people who had learnt how to live in harmony with both time and place, and, perhaps a more difficult thing, with each other.

Time spilt over and bled from one month to the next. Despite being studded by so many celebrations, the overlapping quality of time added a sense of mystery to life here. I felt I would never reach the core, that there was always another layer to be peeled away, belying the place's apparent simplicity. Everyone and everything had a built-in complexity, a truly Latin imprecision alien to northern thinking. Sometimes, the Englishwoman in me retreated, baffled, to consider my lilies and ponder many things in my heart. The true initiates were my children, of whom this youngest would be an Orsolana born and bred.

When we turned in past the cypress trees to the newly gravelled drive, the first thing I saw was grass grown in my absence and, beyond it, all the workmen waiting to greet the new member of their tribe. Maria, who was with me in the car, got out and handed the baby first to Imolo, who took her in his big mutilated hands with infinite care and then passed her on to the hovering Gigi. This was to be Florence's fate in Sant' Orsola, a child loved and shared by many. Imolo was beside himself with pride, both for the baby and for something else. He had tears in his sky-blue eyes.

'Have you seen?' he asked, almost before I had eased myself out of the car.

Then I looked up, and I saw. He had finished the tower and nearly finished the entire façade. He had joined the two halves of the villa, eliminating the gaping chasm that ran down three floors and always gave the house its most ungainly air of dereliction.

'You must have been working nights to get all that done,' I said.

'We have. We did it for the girls, for Isotta and Florence. We'll be ready for the wedding, don't you worry.'